African American Concert Singers Before 1950

African American Concert Singers Before 1950

Darryl Glenn Nettles

McFarland & Company, Inc., Publishers
Jefferson, North Carolina, and London

Library of Congress Cataloguing-in-Publication Data

Nettles, Darryl Glenn.
    African American concert singers before 1950 / Darryl Glenn Nettles.
      p.   cm.
    Includes bibliographical references and index.
    Discography: p.

    ISBN 0-7864-1467-7 (softcover binding : 50# alkaline paper)

    1. Singers—United States—Biography.   2. African American
singers—Biography. I. Title.
ML400.N49   2003
782'.0092'396073—dc21   2003001307

British Library cataloguing data are available

Front cover (foreground): Carol Brice *(Courtesy of the E. Azalia Hackley
Collection, Detroit Public Library) Background and back cover ©2003 Art Today*

Manufactured in the United States of America

*McFarland & Company, Inc., Publishers
  Box 611, Jefferson, North Carolina 28640
    www.mcfarlandpub.com*

To my father, Henry L. Nettles,
a truly great basso and concert artist.
I salute him and his colleagues
with this work.

A Personal Note

William Warfield died on Sunday August 25, 2002, at the Rehabilitation Institute of Chicago, where he had been recovering from a fall. He was 82.

Mr. Warfield was my voice teacher at the University of Illinois, where he was professor of music and chair of the vocal department. In 1994 he joined the faculty at Northwestern University, where he remained until his death.

We students of Mr. Warfield affectionately called him Uncle Bill, for he had a warm and loving relationship with his students. We experienced that love on numerous occasions at his home through meals prepared by Uncle Bill, who was a culinary expert. Tuesday nights I and others from the Warfield vocal studio would gather for what he called family night. One of my favorite menus prepared by Uncle Bill consisted of prime rib, steamed broccoli with almonds and green olives in garlic butter sauce, potato salad, Gooey Butter Cake and double fudge chocolate cake for dessert, and his famous fruit punch which he called the formula. All of this was seasoned with numerous ribald jokes for which Uncle Bill was equally famous.

The mighty voice of this great artist now rings from the heavens with Robeson, Anderson and Hayes. I loved him dearly. He was more than my voice teacher and mentor ... he was my friend.

Darryl Glenn Nettles
September 1, 2002

Acknowledgments

It is impossible to thank every individual who made this work possible. There were just too many people involved in one way or another. As a result, there will be an omission here and there. However, it is my sincerest hope that those persons not listed will understand that I am truly grateful for their concern, interest, and guidance.

There are a few people who must be thanked for deeds performed above and beyond the call of duty. Among them are Rosemary Stevenson, Afro-Americana Bibliographer, the University of Illinois; Dr. John Hill, musicologist, the University of Illinois; William Warfield, renowned concert artist; Agatha Pfeiffer Kalkanis, Music and Performing Arts Department, Detroit Public Library; Salvatore Martirano, professor of composition, the University of Illinois; Charles Holland, concert artist; and Mignon Dunn, professor of voice at the University of Illinois and a performer with the Metropolitan Opera.

There were also numerous friends and colleagues who offered both casual and critical comments, peppered with enthusiasm, that proved to be valuable: Frank Morris, Reynold Scott, Marie Claude des Loges, Drs. Don and Kathy Arnold, Donald L. Hilliard, Dr. Diane Pinderhughes, Felicity Hendricks, Margo Eileen Chaney, and Mr. and Mrs. Thomas Stenhouse.

To my brother, Alan, I am indebted for his wise counsel. To my mother, Julia W. Nettles, I am grateful for her overwhelming surplus of support and encouragement. To my sister, Maryam Ogbu, I am indebted for her instilling in me a powerful admiration of my heritage. To Dr. Christine Perkey, I am thankful for her ability to keep me from giving up as well as for her sound guidance.

Contents

Preface

To what extent have African Americans played a role in the vast world of concert singing? What contributions were made in opera, oratorio, and recital? These are questions that have constantly plagued my mind since I first entered college. One of course hears about Roland Hayes, Marian Anderson, William Warfield, Leontyne Price, and Paul Robeson whenever the question arises. However, there were others. In this book, with the help of articles, reviews, programs, biographical sources, and interviews, I offer a survey of some of the unknown heroes and heroines who paved the way for the post–1950 African American vocal artist. African American performers of the popular music vernacular have received a greater welcome from American society over the years.

Numerous African Americans were involved in the arts as concert singers. Given the times in which they lived and the countless doors that were closed to them, they achieved tremendous results in the face of great adversity. I believe simply presenting information about their careers and experiences can make my point.

As part of my preparation for this work, I scanned numerous issues of magazines and newspapers current to the period of my research. I focused primarily on periodicals with a predominantly African American perspective, such as *The New York Amsterdam News, The Chicago Defender,* and *The New York Age*. These were the news media most likely to cover the achievements of African Americans during the second half of the nineteenth and the first half of the twentieth century.

I am deeply indebted to Mr. Corey Miller, of St. Louis, Missouri, for sharing with me a scrapbook compiled by his grandmother. Mr. Miller's grandmother had a strong sense of ethnic awareness and pride. These feelings motivated her to keep a record of the achievements of African Americans throughout the 1930s and 1940s. Her scrapbook articles offer a wealth of information, often concerning individuals for whom limited printed coverage exists, and many of those articles are reproduced in this work.

My interview with William Warfield serves as an exciting and informative addition to this project. Being an African American concert singer himself, and knowing many of the subjects of my research, he offers valuable insight into the world of concert singing in America for the minority, and helps to shed light on those individuals whose names are scarcely remembered today.

Other books offering information on African American concert singers include Rosalyn M. Story's *And So I Sing: African American Divas of Opera and Concert*; Eileen Southern's *Biographical Dictionary of Afro-American and African Musicians* (1982); and Patricia Turner's *Afro-American Singers: An Index and Preliminary Discography* (1976), to name a few. This book, however, is the first to provide not only biographical information, but quotes from contemporary media (including reviews of concerts) and a discography of the singers' recordings, all in a single source.

The earliest concert singer I've found is Elizabeth Taylor Greenfield. Leontyne Price, Grace Bumbry, Shirley Verret, Vinson Cole, Simon Estes, and others were soon to follow. Their names are as well known as their tremendous contributions and innovations. Their histories are well documented. With William Warfield's New York Town Hall debut in 1950, a new era of vocal contributions by African Americans to the concert and operatic world had begun.

It is my sincere hope that this book will serve as a useful reference source, offering information on a previously neglected aspect of music history. Furthermore, it is my hope that this work will serve as an example of how truly engulfing the artistic world really is, how difficult it has been for minorities in the past, how we have come this far, and where we need to go from here. Perhaps in some small way this project will help to promote the fact that "by knowing more about others we know more about ourselves" (Norman Dello Joio).

Introduction

My father, Henry L. Nettles, is the possessor of a deep, rich bass voice. If given the chance he would have dedicated his life to the world of song. To a certain extent he has. However, he never achieved the acclaim and just rewards a person with his talent truly deserves. To whom do you turn to when you are a teenaged African American in Hartsville, South Carolina, during the Second World War, seeking a career as a concert singer? Are Marian Anderson, Roland Hayes, and Paul Robeson the only African Americans involved in concert singing? Were they the first people of color to strive for success in this field? If not, who came before them? Are opportunities available in Europe for people of color as singers? I've no doubt that these and many additional questions plagued my father while he pursued his ambition. They certainly plagued my mind as I did the same. This work will hopefully shed some light on some of these questions and perhaps, by increasing our awareness, assist in awakening humankind to the true meaning of the arts, a reflection of all of us.

Limited information exists regarding African Americans as performing artists prior to the nineteenth century. During the colonial period they were able to occasionally attend white theaters and apparently demonstrated a love for theater. It is therefore presumed that more activity among people of color took place in the performing arts during this period than we know at present. Before the nineteenth century, grotesque images of African Americans pervaded the white-run artistic community. This should not be surprising, since both slaves and free blacks were a despised

Henry L. Nettles (far right), bass soloist with the Johnson Male Chorus, Buffalo, New York, circa 1954. Courtesy of Henry and Julia Nettles.

minority that had little, if any, influence over the general public. Songs, ballad operas, and other forms of entertainment upheld the dominant sentiment that this minority consisted of piteous, ignorant, and laughable beings.[1]

When Elizabeth Taylor Greenfield (c.1819–1876) and the Fisk Jubilee Singers traveled across the United States and eventually to Europe, in 1853 and 1871 respectively, many white audiences viewed them with a sense of amusement. *Negroes dressed in gowns and tuxedos, singing in concert halls!* Indeed, many reviewers of the day poked fun with their praise concerning the performances of these and other trailblazers. Greenfield, Sissieretta Jones (1869–1933), and other women were said to appear matronly, homely, and frumpy when on stage. Small-minded critics and concertgoers who used the singers' natural features against them as negatives attacked singers with dark hued complexions. How easily the antagonists forgot the appearances of such turn of the century singers as Nellie Melba, Jean de Reszke, Enrico Caruso, and numerous others. They neglected to realize that all, Negroid and Caucasoid, were just people.

The majority of the subjects of my research took advantage of the

European option. Many studied with prominent European vocal instructors of the day. Many embarked upon tours of Europe as members of theatrical touring companies. James Bergen's Star Concert Company, John Isham's Oriental American Company, the Tennessee Concert Company, Black Patti's Troubadours, and Signor A. Farini's Grand Creole and Colored Opera and Concert Company were some of the more popular troupes. These nineteenth century entertainers contradicted the stereotypic images showcased in American minstrelsy of the age. These troupes, composed solely of people of color, often performed scenes from operas and operettas, and featured both popular and recital literature as well. Concert singers, instrumentalists, and comedians joined forces in productions of their own that dealt with their experiences, not those based on the surface features of minstrelsy.[2]

In the late 1890s numerous performers of color migrated to New York City. This migration helped ignite the creation of the first major African American musical comedies. From 1898 to 1915, beginning with *A Trip to Coontown* (1898) by Bob Cole, over thirty shows were produced. These works were written and staged by African Americans and usually featured all-black casts. Many concert singers seeking opera careers found an outlet for their vocal skills in the African American wing of American musical theater. Those who paid their dues during the days of touring companies felt right at home as well. Musical creators such as Bob Cole, J. Rosamund Johnson, Ernest Hogan, Bert Williams, and George Walker helped to keep their singing compatriots busy on the musical stage. Some of their shows revealed their minstrel ancestry, but their importance should not be slighted as a result. The existence of an all African American production was a giant step forward in American show business and a potent tonic for people of color.[3]

American motion pictures of the 1930s brought back the stereotypic portrayals of African Americans from yesteryear. The drive that had taken place in musicals twenty years or so earlier to end such stereotypes was now forgotten. Whites were now writing most of the all-black-cast musicals. One of the most distinctive and controversial works to emerge in the 1930s was George Gershwin's opera *Porgy and Bess* (1935). It perpetuated the usual stereotypic images of African American life found in minstrelsy and yet became a major addition to America's operatic literature due to the talent of the composer. Gershwin insisted that all performances of the work incorporate only people of color in the roles so designated. Such is still the case today. This view, coupled with the beauty of the score, serves as the dominant factor for the opera's support by African American concert singers.

By 1942, after a long battle with the National Association for the Advancement of Colored People, Hollywood's movie moguls agreed to abolish their practice of presenting people of color in stereotyped roles. Furthermore, they agreed to include more realistic characters in movie scripts. The result was a minor change in film and a limited effect on the number of performers of color in predominantly white musicals. However, it did signify a change that was looming on the horizon.[4]

Since the days of Elizabeth Taylor Greenfield and Thomas J. Bowers, recital had played an important part in the lives of African American concert singers. The combined recital experiences of the singers presented in this work literally cover two thirds of the planet. Kimball Hall in Chicago, Jordan Hall in Boston, and the historic Town Hall and Carnegie Hall in New York were particularly important to singers of color. Many a debut took place at these halls. Those in charge of these institutions showed their commitment to artistic talent and potential, regardless of race. They played an important role in the lives of many African Americans and the national artistic community. Their supportive efforts stand as a beacon of courage and a testament to the true oneness the arts symbolize.

With the organization of the Clef Club in 1910, the history of black music in the city of New York entered a new era. The best performers in the city were drawn into the new organization founded by James Reese Europe (1881–1919), and several performance groups were set up, chief among them the Clef Club Orchestra. During the 1911–12 season, white violinist David Mannes and other public-spirited citizens of New York established the Music School Settlement for Colored People, thereby making available for the first time in the history of the nation the opportunity for talented black youngsters to obtain excellent musical training at nominal fees. It should be observed that New York already had a Music School Settlement for whites, which did not accept black students.

During its first year the Music Settlement for Colored [People] combined forces with the Clef Club Orchestra to present a mammoth concert of black music in Carnegie Hall. That practice continued for the next three years, except that the Clef Club Orchestra was replaced by other groups after the 1913 concert. These annual concerts attracted large numbers of music lovers, white and black, and provided occasions for black artists to come before the public, in addition to the school's student groups.[5] Harry T. Burleigh (1866–1949), Roland Hayes (1887–1976), and Marie Selika (1849–1937) were among the leading performers of color called upon to participate.

Landmark opera companies also helped to showcase the operatic skills of African American singers. Mary Cardwell Dawson's National

Negro Opera Company, the Chicago Civic Opera, the Baltimore Civic Opera, the New England Opera, the Aeolian Opera in New York, the New York City Opera, and various European opera houses were instrumental in serving as a strong deterrent to the dominant view that African Americans did not have and did not deserve a place on the operatic stage.

In the second half of the twentieth century the Imperial Opera Company, the National Negro Opera Company, the Harlem Opera Company, Opera South, the Houston Opera Ebony Guild, Onyx Opera Atlanta, and Opera Ebony were formed. Many of these companies no longer exist today. Onyx Opera Atlanta and Opera Ebony have been more successful than most.

Onyx Opera Atlanta was founded in 1988 by Laura English-Robinson, soprano; Uzee Brown, Jr., bass-baritone; and Oral Moses, bass. Performers and selected works are not exclusively African American. Their repertoire includes the works of Wm. Grant Still, Scott Joplin, Samuel Coleridge-Taylor, Mozart, Bizet, and Puccini.

Benjamin Matthews and Sister Mary Elise S.B.S. Sanders founded Opera Ebony in 1973. Opera Ebony has performed at New York's Lincoln Center, Carnegie Hall and Philadelphia's Academy of Music. The company has also performed in Brazil, Estonia, Russia, Sweden, Finland, Switzerland, and Fort-de-France, Martinique. The longest surviving African American Opera Company in American history is Opera Ebony.

Prominent teachers such as Arthur Hubbard, Jean de Reszke, and Rosa Ponselle took many singers into their studios when it was not the most popular thing to do. They were people of integrity.

In years past, the image of the African American in the arts was less than exalted. Many talented individuals were prejudged to be inferior within the dominant Anglo-American culture. However, the world of opera, recital, film, and musical theater provided opportunities for employment and served as an outlet for talent, thus helping to enlighten the open-minded and those with creative imaginations throughout the world.

The great tenor Charles Holland (1909–1987) once shared a story with me concerning his first encounter with Louis B. Mayer, the movie mogul of Metro-Goldwyn-Mayer (MGM). Mr. Holland was in Hollywood making films with the Hall Johnson chorus. While in Hollywood his voice came to Mr. Mayer's attention. Mayer said to him, "If you were white I could make a million dollars off you." Another individual once said to Holland after an audition, "Come back as soon as you change color."[6]

There are more African American concert singers in the world today than ever before. However, while the number of successful females of color has increased steadily since the days of Marian Anderson, the number of successful males is still rather small. No one can deny that improvements have taken place for both sexes. However, the void between African American males and females seems rather wide, even in this day and age. What can the reason or reasons be behind this troubling phenomenon?

Says singer Simon Estes, "I don't do much singing in my own country. I work in Europe: at La Scala, in Paris, in London, in Berlin, in Hamburg, Vienna.... If I were to ask you to name me five African American men singing in leading roles you would have [a] problem."[7]

Is racism still rampant in the world of opera today? Some singers, such as Shirley Verrett, Barbara Hendricks, Vinson Cole, and Grace Bumbry, have said they've never encountered racial prejudice. Miss Bumbry also said that while giving a series of recitals in the American South of the 1960s she didn't come across any animosity of any sort. Perhaps she forgot about her *Tannhäuser* debacle at Bayreuth in 1961. Richard Wagner's grandsons, Wolfgang and Wieland, engaged Bumbry for the role of Venus in *Tannhäuser*. So many people were angry, and voiced their resentment, that Wieland Wagner had a change of heart. As soon as a white woman came along with the ability to sing the role better than Bumbry, he would most assuredly hire her. Were his words merely a device to soothe the tempers of the angry people or did he really believe what he'd said? Regardless of his beliefs, there is no question about what the vast majority of Bayreuth enthusiasts felt.

Soprano Jessye Norman's opinion differs from the aforementioned singers. She believes prejudice exists, especially on the management level, and is rather skeptical about the future. According to Miss Norman, management tends to be conservative, often saying one thing while in essence feeling another.

Can racial discrimination stand in the way of a major artist? Perhaps not, to a certain extent. For the budding artist, however, it may be a different story. The key may be to have more minorities on decision-making levels. Then there will perhaps be an improvement.[8]

Simon Estes: "In all our opera companies, there are no Blacks in decision-making roles. In the United States we have been able to be performers, but we can't be the managers, directors, owners. To my knowledge, I don't know of any Blacks who make decisions about policy at the Metropolitan Opera, or any other companies. There are no Black artist managers, no Black critics. Now, I don't state it with bitterness, I state it with sadness. I hope we'll be able to reduce these problems eventually."[9]

Some have said that the problem of casting males is not due to race, but due to professional standards. Few African American males are prepared to handle professional opera as well as concert works and recitals.

William Warfield vehemently disagrees. He often remarked to me of the talented male singers he encountered at numerous universities and conservatories across the country, including the University of Illinois during his tenure there. Mr. Warfield also questions the "high international standards" of many non–African American individuals in the field who have been successful. Someone once said, "Fame is an accident that is sometimes accompanied by talent." The same can be said of one succeeding in opera, regardless of the level of one's ability. Peter G. Davis and other noted critics have taken many professional singers to task for their lack of preparedness and skill.

Perhaps the answer is clear when viewed from a sexual standpoint. Soprano Ellen Faull and tenor George Shirley believe that most audiences view the teaming of white men with black women on stage without much thought and certainly not as a threat. However, they find the reverse, a black man with a white woman, to be extremely threatening. The result being that male dominance is controlled by sex, and the black man, complete with the visual stereotypes, thereby threatens the power of the white man by performing opposite a white woman.

Simon Estes: "Opera is highly sophisticated, dignified, social. It's been an area where Blacks have not been allowed to participate. The doors have been more open since Marian Anderson — but when she gave her Met debut, she was a bit past her prime, and she could hardly be an effective singer. The doors really came down with Leontyne Price — she was a woman, she was not a threat in the male dominated, administrative world. It just doesn't make sense that one gender can sing, and the other can't."[10]

Several times throughout his career, Mr. Shirley had engagements for roles in Germany canceled at the last minute. [11] Such has been the case for Mr. Estes as well.

"You know," says Estes, "it's very strange, if we try to show we are strong, and if we are not just going to be sheep following a blind leader, we have to admit that these problems have existed. [If] their their talents are equal, they'd take the white singer. If the Black singer is better, they'll still take the White singer. But if the Black singer is a lot better — they'll hire him, but pay him less."[12]

A term quite common in theater today is "color-blind casting." It's opposite would be "dramatic realism." Which road should opera boards take? Leona Mitchell, soprano, once had the role of Donna Anna in Mozart's *Don Giovanni* swept away from her for a Glyndebourne Opera production. The director, Peter Brook, thought her being an African American would detract from the opera's realism. Perhaps Mr. Brook didn't realize that non–African American Carmens have often been fat, Canios short, Romeos and Juliettes over forty years of age, and Otellos and Aidas played by performers of non–African descent. [13]

Simon Estes: "When I sing in Europe, they treat me in the opera houses the same way they treat Placido Domingo in this country. I'm not going to say that racism does not exist in Europe. But it exists far less there than in my own country. When I sing in Hamburg, Berlin, Paris, the people don't care about my skin color. They engage me because I can do the part. When I sang in *Don Carlo*, I made myself up a little lighter. But since that time, I haven't made myself up light. They only care 'is he qualified, can he sing, can he act.' I hope that happens in our country, I certainly feel like the forgotten American sometimes."[14]

Another argument used to explain the lack of men of color in opera is the lack of male singers with the vocal calibre to match the successful African American woman in opera. Is it a lack of top vocal calibre or a lack of awareness regarding the sound of African Americans? Is there a "black voice?" Many would say yes. Luciano Pavarotti, Placido Domingo, and others have used such terms as dusky, smoky, dark, warm, burgundy-colored, mellow, etc. One doesn't aurally have difficulty identifying Italian, German, Nordic, and Russian voices, so why not include African American voices as well? [15]

Doctors have been unable to find a physiological difference between blacks and whites concerning vocal cords, chest and throat cavity size, etc. Soprano Judith Raskin thinks the vocal differences may stem from culture. Mezzo-Soprano Betty Allen agrees with this view, citing the use of language inflections as the key to understanding why one can label a singer's ethnic background.[16]

African Americans, and indeed all humankind, have benefited from the ever-increasing acceptance and admiration of African American artists from generation to generation. They have helped to disprove the old stereotypes that lingered for so long in our society. The singers covered in this humble effort will be remembered not only as concert singers of color, but also as artists who gave their rich individuality to the world at large.

Notes

1. Bordman, *American Musical Theatre: A Chronicle* (New York: Oxford University Press, 1978); Odell, *Annals of the New York Stage*, 15 vols. (New York: Columbia University Press, 1927–1949); and Southern, *The Music of Black Americans*, 2nd ed. (New York: Norton, 1983).

2. *Folio* 19 (December 1880): 453; the Baltimore *Afro-American*, 1892– (from 1901 to 1916 titled the *Afro-American Ledger*); and *Crisis*, 1910–1940.

3. A large clipping file is preserved in scrapbook form in the Billy Rose Theatre Collection, New York Public Library, and Lincoln Center.

4. Cripps, *Slow Fade to Black: The Negro in American Film, 1900–1942* (New York: Oxford University Press, 1977). A folder of reviews of *The Southerners* can be found in the Harvard Theatre Collection.

5. Southern, "In Retrospect: Black-Music Concerts at Carnegie Hall, 1912–15" *The Black Perspective in Music,* Volume 6, Number 1, New York, 1978.

6. This was taken from a backstage conversation with Mr. Holland during a rehearsal in Hill Auditorium at the University of Michigan in 1984.

7. "Interview with Simon Estes," *Classical Music in Black and White*, Indiana University, 15 September 2000.

8. Schonberg, "A Bravo for Opera's Black Voices," *The New York Times Magazine,* January 17, 1982, sec. 6.

9. "Interview with Simon Estes," *Classical Music in Black and White*, Indiana University 15 September 2000.

10. Ibid.

11. Schonberg, "A Bravo for Opera's Black Voices," *The New York Times Magazine,* January 17, 1982, sec. 6.

12. "Interview with Simon Estes," *Classical Music in Black and White*, Indiana University, 15 September 2000.

13. Schonberg, "A Bravo for Opera's Black Voices," *The New York Times Magazine,* January 17, 1982, sec. 6.

14. "Interview with Simon Estes," *Classical Music in Black and White*, Indiana University, 15 September 2000.

15. Schonberg, "A Bravo for Opera's Black Voices," *The New York Times Magazine,* January 17, 1982, sec. 6.

16. Ibid.

THE SINGERS

Marian Anderson
(1897–1993)

Numerous concert and operatic singers of various races and different generations have hailed Marian Anderson as their primary influence and sole inspiration for entering the world of music and seeking a singing career. William Warfield, Mignon Dunn, Leontyne Price, Shirley Verrett, Grace Bumbry, Kathleen Battle and Jesseye Norman have expressed their love and admiration for Miss Anderson countless times throughout their careers. In her prime, her contralto voice was deep and rich. She was not the first African American to embark on a career as a concert singer; however, she was the first to achieve true celebrity status across the western world, coupled with great respect. According to her birth certificate, she was born on February 27, 1897, in Philadelphia, Pennsylvania. Tenor Roland Hayes and Anderson's church community gave her financial support and critical guidance as her talent developed. Recalling being turned away from a local music school by a young admissions clerk, Anderson said:

> I don't think I said a word. I just looked at this girl and was shocked that such words could come from one so young. If she had been old and sour-faced I might not have been startled. I cannot say why her youth shocked me as much as her words. On second thought, I could not conceive of a person surrounded as she was with the joy that is music without having some sense of its beauty and understanding rub off on her. I did not argue with her or ask to see her superior. It was as if a cold, horrifying hand had been laid on me. I turned and walked out.

She studied with Giuseppe Boghetti and made her New York Town Hall debut in 1924. Her discomfort with foreign languages was made apparent during her recital. Threatening to end her career, Boghetti advised her to continue her training. Anderson went to London in 1925 and studied and performed throughout Europe for the next ten years. She sang before many of Europe's leading dignitaries and musicians, including the Archbishop of Salzburg, the noted conductor Arturo Toscanini, and composers Jean Sibelius and Roger Quilter. In 1935 Anderson returned to New York's Town Hall and gave a recital that was a critical success.

Anderson made headlines and the history books when her manager Sol Hurok and officials from Howard University attempted to have Anderson perform at Constitution Hall in Washington, D. C. The Daughters of the American Revolution (DAR), the owners of the hall, refused to extend their permission. The First Lady, Eleanor Roosevelt, resigned as a member in protest. The DAR's refusal, coupled with the resignation of Mrs. Roosevelt, created a media frenzy. The Department of the Interior, along with Mrs. Roosevelt, scheduled the concert on the steps of the Lincoln Memorial on April 9, 1939. The first piece Marian Anderson presented on that eventful day in front of the Lincoln statue was "My Country 'Tis of Thee, Sweet Land of Liberty, of Thee I Sing."

She debuted at the Metropolitan Opera as Ulrica in Verdi's *Un Ballo in Maschera* in 1954. She was past her prime by that time, but her presence, in place of a younger African American artist at that historic time, gave the occasion more meaning and significance.

Anderson was awarded the Spingarn Award in 1938 by President Roosevelt, and the Presidential Medal of Freedom in 1963 by President Johnson. She also performed at the inaugurations of Presidents Eisenhower and Kennedy. Her nephew, noted conductor James DePriest, conducted the orchestra for her final concert in 1965. She died of congestive heart failure on April 8, 1993, in Portland, Oregon.

SOURCES

Abdul, Raoul, *Blacks in Classical Music: A Personal History* (New York: Dodd, Mead, 1978).

Anderson, Marian, *My Lord, What a Morning* (New York: Viking Press, 1956).

Koznin, Allan, "Marian Anderson Is Dead at 96; Singer Shattered Racial Barriers," *New York Times*, 9 April 1993, A20.

Smith, Eric Ledell, *Blacks in Opera: An Encyclopedia of People and Companies, 1873–1993* (Jefferson, N.C.: McFarland, 1994).

Ralph Banks

A native of Pittsburgh, Pennsylvania, Ralph Banks had a promising but all too brief concert career. His vocal training in Pittsburgh led him to study extensively in Italy. Upon his return to the United States, Banks gave his first professional recital on November 15, 1929, at Steinway Hall in New York. At this time, he was under the management of Arthur Judson. His song recital was quite successful, with reviewers noting his refined style, command of languages, and choice of repertory. Ralph Banks, baritone, died shortly thereafter.

SOURCES

Cuney-Hare, Maud, *Negro Musicians and Their Music* (Washington, D.C.: Da Capo Press, 1936), 383.

Flora Batson Bergen
(1864–1906)

Flora Batson, soprano, was born on April 16, 1864, in Washington, D.C. At the age of three she moved to Providence, Rhode Island, and sang throughout the area as a child. She began appearing in local concerts in Boston, Massachusetts, and Providence in the 1880s. She joined James Bergen's Star Concert Company in 1885 as a last-minute replacement for soprano Nellie Brown. The Bergen Company was scheduled to appear in Providence, and Nellie Brown was forced to cancel her appearance due to prior performance commitments in the South. Batson was already quite well known throughout the Providence area and greatly impressed James Bergen. He eventually took over her management, made her the leading soprano of his company, and married her in 1887. Bergen was an Anglo-American. Batson had successful debut appearances in 1885 in Philadelphia and New York. After her marriage to Bergen she toured a great deal. From 1887 to 1896 she made three international tours. Her audiences included Queen Victoria of England, Pope Leo XIII, Queen Lil of Hawaii, the royal family of New Zealand, and many others. She also went to Africa. She toured with bass Gerard Miller in 1896 after leaving her husband. The singers were featured performers with the "South Before the War Company." Their act was entitled "Operatic Specialties." From 1899 to 1900 Batson and Miller toured Australia with the "Orpheus McAdoo Minstrels and Vaudeville Company." Flora Batson had a wide vocal range that covered the baritone register as well as the soprano register. As a result, she was known as "the Double-Voiced Queen of Song." Critics and public alike held her in the highest regard as an African American concert singer, placing her among such giants as M. Sissieretta Jones, Marie Selika, and the incomparable Elizabeth Taylor Greenfield. Virginia Montgomery, of New York, was her favorite accompanist. Flora Batson died suddenly on December 1, 1906, in Philadelphia.

SOURCES

Cuney-Hare, Maud, *Negro Musicians and Their Music* (Washington, D.C.: Da Capo Press, 1936), 219–220.
De Lerma, Dominique-René, *The New Grove Dictionary of American Music* (New York: St. Martin's Press, 1986), Vol. 1, 160.
Southern, Eileen, *Biographical Dictionary of Afro-American and African Musicians* (Westport, CT: Greenwood Press, 1982), 30.

"Personal," *The New York Age*, 24 October 1891

Ever since she appeared here a half decade ago in ballad parts, Flora Batson has been a prime favorite. Had she been content with such a small reputation as satisfies the average cantatrice she would be singing ballad parts still; but she was not so content. She has been a hard and conscientious student of voice, method, and stage presence. As a consequence her voice has gained in flexibility and strength, which her mastery of technique enables her to use to the best advantage. In the two concerts given in New York and Brooklyn recently, Miss Batson astonished the audiences with a bit of acting in the "Bridge Song" whose dramatic effect was decidedly acceptable and appreciable. It was a decided hit. To those who remember how awkward Miss Batson used to be on the stage, the self-possessed displayed in this particular song, and in her general appearance, was in the nature of a revelation. Hard study will tell in the work of an artist and it tells very perceptibly in the work of Miss Batson.

"Flora Batson Bergen; Story of Her Career and a Tribute to James G. Bergen," *The New York Age*, 27 December 1906

[Philadelphia] The sudden death of Flora Batson-Bergen recalls with vividness the concert furor of 20 years ago. She came to Philadelphia widely heralded, and the amusement and music loving among us were all agog to hear her. Her first essay was at Musical Fund Hall, and by reason of the advertising methods employed the interest was sustained to the extent of having the Academy of Music. Flora Batson had a peculiar voice, both as to range and quality, and, although untutored, she possessed a manner, which lent value to her work as a singer. Bergen, a New England manager, saw a gold mine in Flora Batson and started a concert scheme, covering many cities, built on unique lines of management. He offered premiums in money, and ticket selling became a fad, mostly by church members, who worked zealously to add to the coffers of their respective churches. Bergen lived up to his pledges and never once defaulted, either in a promise after that fashion or in his amusements. Later on he married his protégé, who became stepmother to a white son by a prior marriage. Flora Batson's style seemed to meet the desires of the average public, who put her on a pedestal, where she held sway for many years. Bergen's plan was to encourage home talent, at whatever place his star was billed to sing, and, not only that, but whenever he heard of skilled talent, [he] gave the chance for its exploitation. In this, Philadelphia's worth got recognition. Among his presentations were Lois L. Brown, Richard Strange and the Amphion Singing Society; Emory Jones and his wife, Madame Saville-Jones, were put on for hearings. Madame Virginia Montgomery of New York was usually the accompanist for Flora Batson. It is within the memory of scores the advent of a Baltimore male chorus. After a while new fields were explored. Then Bergen died, and his wife was left without inheritance and had to depend upon her own resources. Flora Batson was a profitable drawing card, and it is sad to think how [much] of the financial success she made was diverted out of her hands. In many aspects her career was greater than that of any other singer since the days of the Black Swan, whose real career, like that of Flora Batson's began in this city.

Jules Bledsoe
(1898–1943)

I had always thought that he was the reason that *[Old Man River]* was in E flat, because [I was told that] he was actually a heldentenor, but [when I heard him it] didn't sound like a real high voice. And [I was told] he used to go up to a high note at the end in *Old Man River*. B flat I think it was, but the recording he made didn't do that at all. It sounded like just an ordinary baritone range voice, but I had heard from people who tried to describe him to me that he was sort of a high tenor. So in the *Old Man River* the lowest note written was a B flat, but that was not what he did on the record. It sounded low. Now it could possibly be that that was later. That record was made later in life, but he still didn't sound like a heldentenor. It sounded like a straight baritone to me ... His voice to me sounded more or less like the Todd Duncan type of baritone.

— *William Warfield, April 21, 1994*

Jules (Julius) Bledsoe, baritone, was born on December 29, 1898, in Waco, Texas. As a child he studied the piano and sang in church concerts. He received his A.B. degree in 1918 from Bishop College in Marshall, Texas. From 1918 to 1919 he attended Virginia Union College in Richmond, Virginia, and Columbia University Medical School from 1919 to 1924. In addition to his medical study, Bledsoe studied voice with Claude Warford, Parisolti, and Lazar Samoilofff. By the time of his debut in 1924 at New York's Aeolian Hall, Bledsoe abandoned his medical career and set his sights on music. For his debut he was under the management of Sol Hurok. In 1926 he sang in Frank Harling's opera *Deep River*. It was the first opera to be given with a mixed cast in the United States. The year 1927 brought Bledsoe the opportunity to play what would be the most famous role of his career and the chance to introduce one of the most famous songs in the history of American Musical Theater. The role was that of Joe in Jerome Kern's *Show Boat*, and the song was "Ol' Man River." Ziegfeld produced *Show Boat* for its Broadway premiere, in which Bledsoe took part, and Bledsoe also toured with the show in Europe. He sang the role for the 1929 film version. Bledsoe was also the first African American artist to be employed continuously by a Broadway theater. He was appointed to the music staff of the Roxy Theater in 1927. They broadcasted regularly over the airwaves as Roxy's Gang. In 1931 he toured Europe as a recitalist. From 1932 to 1934 he attracted attention to a certain degree as an opera interpreter. He sang the role of Amonasro in Verdi's *Aida* in 1932 in Cleveland for Lawrence Productions, the title role of *Boris Godunov* by Moussorgsky in 1933 at the Italian Opera in Holland, Amonasro in *Aida* once again for the Chicago Opera Company under the management of Alfred Salmaggi in 1933, and the title role in Louis Gruenberg's *The Emperor Jones* at the Municipal Theatre in Amsterdam in 1934. Maestro Parenti conducted the performances, which also took place in Paris, Vienna, Milan, Brussels, and London.

For the British Broadcasting Company (BBC) he programmed "Songs of the Negro," a special series. The following year he appeared in the London production of *Blackbirds of 1936* by Lew Leslie. In 1942 he made his second film, *Drums of the Congo*. Jules Bledsoe was a composer and an early recording artist, in addition to his other endeavors. His great versatility and artistry earned him a sense of respect and loyalty from critics and colleagues second only to Roland Hayes. His most famous composition was the *African Suite* for violin and orchestra. Bishop College bestowed upon him an honorary doctorate in 1941. Jules Bledsoe died in Hollywood, California, on July 14, 1943.

SOURCES

Cuney-Hare, Maud, *Negro Musicians and Their Music* (Washington, D.C.: Da Capo Press, 1936), 358–362.

De Lerma, Dominique-René, *The New Grove Dictionary of American Music* (New York: St. Martin's Press, 1986), Vol. 1, 233.

Southern, Eileen, *Biographical Dictionary of Afro-American and African Musicians* (Westport, CT: Greenwood Press, 1982), 38–39.

New York Amsterdam News, 10 February 1940:

Jules Bledsoe, internationally famous baritone, who gave a brilliant recital at Town Hall recently, will sing at the Heywood Braun memorial service sponsored by the Newspaper Guild at Manhattan Center on February 12.

After a much too lengthy absence from the local concert stage, Jules Bledsoe, internationally famous baritone and creator of the "Ol' Man River" role in "Showboat," sang to a packed house at Town Hall last Sunday night in his second appearance since he returned from a European tour two years ago.

Obviously singing over a heavy cold, Mr. Bledsoe offered an unusually brilliant and varied program which splendidly displayed his wide range and multiple talents. Of particular interest was his group of "Songs of Freedom and Hope" which were "dedicated to the victims of radical religious and political persecution ..." Included in these were Sibelius' "War Song of Tyrtaeus," Dvorak's "Biblical Song," Cherniavsky's "The Kaddish of My Ancestry," and Mr. Bledsoe's own stirring composition of Countee Cullen's "Pagan Prayer" which was impressively done.

The program opened with Bononcini's "Per La Gloria d'Adoravi," Beethoven's "In Questa Tomba," and arias by Mozart and Donizetti (all in Italian). But Mr. Bledsoe really began to warm up with the French group, of which Debussy's "Mandoline," "Chanson Triste" by DuParc, and Fourdrain's "Chevauches Cosaque" were excellent. Mr. Bledsoe is, without a doubt, at his best in German lieder which was obvious in his warm interpretation of Wolf's "Gesang Weyla's," Schubert's "Der Blinde Knabe" and "Der Erlkonig," and Schumann's "Ich Grolle Nicht." His program closed with the traditional Negro spirituals, which included "O Mary!

Where Is Yo' Baby?" "What a Tryin' Time," "Der's a Man Goin' Round Takin' Names," and the singer's own arrangement of "Go Down, Moses!"

There were several encores which included Langston Hughes' "Sad Song in the Air" (music by Jacques Wolf), "Deep River," "Ol' Man River," and the very popular "Shortnin' Bread" in the delivery of which Mr. Bledsoe certainly has no equal. Sanford Schlussel was an able accompanist.

Mr. Bledsoe's next appearance in New York will be as soloist at the Heywood Braun memorial sponsored by the Newspaper Guild at Manhattan Center on Monday evening, February 12.

"Jules Bledsoe Sings in Town Hall," *Musical America*, 10 February 1940, 259

Jules Bledsoe, baritone. Sanford Schlussel, accompanist. The Town Hall, January 28, evening.

Mr. Bledsoe has long been known as the possessor of one of the finest voices of the Negro race. Who does not remember his sonorous "Ol' Man Ribber" in "Show Boat" as well as a beautiful song recital in the Town Hall in the middle twenties. A sojourn in France since then has altered his style considerably and whether this is for the better, or not, is a matter of taste. The voice itself has been lifted in tessitura with the result that the scale is not invariably even and certain notes at the extremes of the scale were produced with evident effort. Interpretatively speaking, it was in songs with a direct appeal that the singer's work was most effective. D'Indy's "Lied Maritime" was especially well given and the Dvorak "Biblical Song" was also excellent. The Spirituals were sung with the authentic atmosphere.

Edward Boatner
(1898–1981)

Edward Boatner of course was in New York, and, as a matter of fact, Robert Guillaume studied with Edward Boatner. And he told me [Edward Boatner] had a studio up in Harlem, I understand, and he was quite caustic. Not in a nasty way, but Robert went to study with him, [Edward Boatner] said, "Um hm! Now what do you want to do?"

ROBERT GUILLAUME: "I want to study with you."
EDWARD BOATNER: "Um hm! You gone down there with the white folks and ruined your voice. Now you come up here and let me straighten you out. Huh? Well, let's get to work!"

He was a really spicy guy ... A lot of people went and worked with him and I understand he was a wonderful coach.

— *William Warfield, April 21, 1994*

Edward Boatner was a man of many talents. He was active in the artistic arena as a composer, arranger, choral director, vocal instructor, and concert baritone. He was born on November 13, 1898, in New Orleans, Louisiana. Boatner's father was an itinerant minister who pastored numerous churches throughout his lifetime. Boatner, along with his family, accompanied his father on his travels from church to church. The singing that Boatner encountered at various churches greatly impressed him and led him to begin collecting spirituals at an early age. Due to the constant resettlement of his family, Boatner's education encompassed many areas, including St. Louis, Missouri; Kansas City, Kansas; Western University in Quintaro, Kansas; the Boston Conservatory of Music in Massachusetts; and the Chicago College of Music in Illinois, where he received his Bachelor of Music degree in 1932. Numbered among his teachers are Louis Victor Saar, Felix Deyo, and Rudolph Schramm.

Two African American musical giants of the day played important roles in the development of Boatner's career — concert tenor Roland Hayes and pianist-composer R. Nathaniel Dett. Hayes encouraged Boatner to study voice after hearing him sing in Kansas. Dr. Dett worked with Boatner as his protégé. He coached Boatner and concertized with Boatner throughout the New England states.

After residing in Boston (1917–c1925), Boatner settled in Chicago. While there he directed community choral ensembles, served as a church organist-choir master, and continued his concert singing. From 1925 to 1931 he served as director of music for the National Baptist Convention and served as director of music at Samuel Houston College in Austin, Texas, in 1933. He later taught and served as dean in Marshal, Texas, at the Wiley College. He then resided in New York in the late 1930s. This would prove to be his permanent home. In New York Boatner continued working with church and community musical organizations. The noted actor Robert Guillaume was one of the members of his vocal studio.

Edward Boatner's fame is primarily due to his efforts as an arranger of spirituals. Great African American concert artists of the day, such as H.T. Burleigh, Marian Anderson, and Roland Hayes, introduced many of Boatner's pieces. Mr. Boatner published his first arrangement, "Give Me Jesus," in 1918. In addition to his collections of spirituals, he published his *Book of 30 Choral Afro-American Spirituals, Sixteen Solo Spirituals for*

Voice and Piano, Spiritual Triumphant Old and New and a piano manual. Boatner also composed a musical comedy, *Julius Sees Her; Freedom Suite,* for orchestra, chorus, and narrator; and an Afro-American "spiritual musical," *The Man from Nazareth.*

Two of his children, Adelaide and Clifford, became concert artists. His other son, Edward "Sonny" Stitt, became a famous jazz artist.

Edward Boatner died on June 16, 1981, in New York City.

SOURCES

Obituary: *The Black Perspective in Music,* Vol. 9, No. 2, 239.
Southern, Eileen, *Biographical Dictionary of Afro-American and African Musicians* (Westport, Connecticut: Greenwood Press, 1982), 39.

"Harlem Varieties Program Proves Newest Radio Hit,"
***New York Amsterdam News,* 18 February 1939, 3**

"Harlem Varieties," crack radio program presented by the Amsterdam News every Sunday afternoon from 3 to 4 o'clock over station WHOM appears destined to become a permanent feature as the program scored tremendously with its second broadcast on Lincoln's Birthday.

Grouped together as the stellar attraction of the program last Sunday were Orlando Robeson, tenor; Joel A. Rogers, author, historian and world traveler; Professor Edward Boatner and his Concord Baptist Church choir, each a star in his own right.

McHenry Boatwright
(1928–1994)

McHenry Boatwright was born in Tennile, Georgia, on February 29, 1928. At the New England Conservatory of Music he received a Bachelor of Music Degree in piano in 1950 and a Bachelor of Music Degree in voice in 1954. He received Marian Anderson awards in 1953 and 1954. The noted bass-baritone made his formal concert debut in 1956 in Boston. Two years later he made his New York debut. That same year he made his operatic debut with the New England Opera Theater in the role of Arkel in Debussy's *Pelleas et Melisande.* He created the central role in Schuller's opera *The Visitation* on October 12, 1966, in Hamburg. He repeated the role at the Metropolitan Opera when the opera made its debut.

Sarah Sedgwick Bowers

Known as "the colored Nightingale," Sarah Sedgwick Bowers continued a musical tradition deeply rooted in the Bowers family. Her brother, John C. Bowers (1811–1873), was an organist at St. Thomas African Episcopal Church in Philadelphia. Her other brother, Thomas Bowers, was a concert tenor.

Sarah began touring as a professional concert soprano in 1856. She later organized a touring concert company.

SOURCES

Southern, Eileen, *Biographical Dictionary of Afro-American and African Musicians* (Westport, CT: Greenwood Press, 1982), 42–43.

Thomas J. Bowers
(c. 1823–1885)

Thomas J. Bowers, tenor, was born in Philadelphia, Pennsylvania. From his older brother, John C. Bowers (1811–1873), he received his early musical training. His older brother taught him organ and piano, and at the age of eighteen, Thomas succeeded his brother John as organist of St. Thomas African Episcopal Church in Philadelphia. He later studied voice with the renowned Elizabeth Taylor Greenfield. He appeared with Greenfield in recital at the Samson Street Hall in 1854 in Philadelphia. Critics soon called him the "American Mario" and the "Colored Mario," comparing him to Giovanni Matteo Mario, one of the most celebrated Italian tenors of the day. Eventually, Colonel J.H. Wood became his manager, and Bowers and Greenfield toured Canada and parts of the United States. For his Hamilton, Ontario, appearance a party of six people of color was told they could not occupy the first-class seats for which they had purchased tickets. Bowers as a result refused to appear before this or any other concert before a segregated audience. Another step toward progress had been set.

In 1964 the noted African American actor William Marshall portrayed Thomas Bowers in an episode on the television series *Bonanza*. Bowers died on October 3, 1885, in Philadelphia.

SOURCES

Cuney-Hare, Maud, *Negro Musicians and Their Music* (Washington, D.C.: Da Capo Press, 1936), 199–201.

De Lerma, Dominique-René, *The New Grove Dictionary of American Music* (New York, St. Martin's Press: 1986), Vol. 1, 280.

Southern, Eileen, *Biographical Dictionary of Afro-American and African Musicians* (Westport, CT: Greenwood Press, 1982), 42–43.

Carol Brice
(1918–1985)

Now Carol and I, we were very good friends. I'd known Carol through the years and when I first did *Porgy and Bess*, with the 1952 company that

the State Department sent to Vienna and Berlin, Carol Brice was the *Mariah*. And she was an excellent *Mariah*. [This was] the first time I'd heard anybody do the *I hate your guts* ... She was just fabulous in that. And with Robert Guillaume who was the *Sportin' Life*. We did that in Munich together at the Volksoper and Carol at that time had had a very stormy personal life. Well, to put it very frankly, she was an abused wife. She refused to leave [her husband], her husband died, and all that stuff. And then she met Thomas

Portrait of Carol Brice. Courtesy of the E. Azalia Hackley Collection, Detroit Public Library.

Carey, who was also over in Europe at that time, and they fell in love. And for the first time in her life she knew what tender loving care was from a man. She was just like a sixteen-year-old bride. It was just wonderful seeing *that* Carol come to the surface. And she sang gorgeously.

Carol was pretty active right up — you know she died from cancer. And when the Metropolitan put on the *Porgy and Bess* for the first time, with Simon Estes and Grace Bumbry, they invited a lot of us who had been connected with *Porgy and Bess* to be at the performance. And one of the people that was at that performance was Carol Brice, and at that time she was in a wheelchair. And she said, "I want to be there. I'm going to be there even if I have to go in a wheelchair." And it was not long after that that she passed away. "Now I've seen it come to the Met."

— *William Warfield, April 21, 1994*

Carol Brice, contralto, was born on April 16, 1918, in Sedalia, North Carolina. Her brothers, Jonathan and Eugene, were also skilled musicians. Eugene was a professional bass-baritone and Jonathan was a highly skilled pianist. The three siblings often toured as the Brice trio. Carol Brice studied at the Palmer Memorial Institute in Sedalia, North Carolina; received a Bachelor of Music degree in 1939 from Talladega College in Alabama; and attended the Juilliard School of Music in New York from 1939–1944, where she received a professional diploma in voice. At the Juilliard School she worked with the legendary Bill "Bojangles" Robinson in the Mike Todd production of *The Hot Mikado* at the New York World's Fair in 1939. She also worked with the equally legendary Harry (Henry) Thacker Burleigh when she served as a soloist at St. George's Episcopal Church in New York from 1939 to 1943. H.T. Burleigh was baritone soloist for the church from 1894 to 1946. She performed at President Franklin Roosevelt's third inaugural concert in 1941, and in 1943 became the first African American to win the coveted Walter Naumburg Award. That same year she made her New York recital debut at the Chaplet. Two years later she made her New York Town Hall debut. Countless recitals and concerts followed in the United States, Europe, and South America. Brice presented a recital on television in 1945 for the Columbia Broadcasting System (CBS), and appeared with the symphony orchestras of Pittsburgh in 1945, Boston in 1946, and San Francisco in 1948.

Carol Brice appeared in Clarence Cameron White's opera *Ouanga* in 1956, Blitzstein's opera *Regina* in 1960, *Saratoga* by Arlen in 1960, Jerome Kern's *Show Boat* in 1961, and Gershwin's opera *Porgy and Bess* in 1961 and 1976. She appeared at the Vienna Volksoper from 1967 to 1971 in *Porgy and Bess*, *Show Boat*, and *Carousel*. Her husband, baritone Thomas Carey, and she joined the voice faculty of the University of Oklahoma at Norman in 1974. Together they established the Cimarron Circuit Opera Company. Carol Brice died on February 15, 1985.

SOURCES

De Lerma, Dominique-René, *The New Grove Dictionary of American Music* (New York: St. Martin's Press, 1986), Vol. 1, 292.
Eileen, Southern, *Biographical Dictionary of Music and Musicians* (Westport, CT: Greenwood Press, 1982), 47.

"Carol Brice, Contralto (Debut)," *Musical America,* 25 March 1945, 22.

Carol Brice, Negro contralto, the first of her race to receive a reward from the Naumburg Foundation, gave her prize recital in the Town Hall on the afternoon of March 13. Miss Brice exhibited a voice of large volume and agreeable quality. She also disclosed possibilities in the field of interpretative singing, which though not as yet fully realized are definitely promising. Three airs from Handel's "Hercules" began the program and these were followed by two Franz songs, of which "Im Herbst" was the better, and Schubert "Der Erlkonig" which while not consistently excellent, had moments of effectiveness. Bemberg's treacly "La Mort de Jeanne d'Arc" had obviously had more work put upon it than its inherent qualities merit. Respighi's "Nebbie" was well done and there were songs in English and the inevitable Spirituals at the end. Excellent accompaniments were played by the singer's brother, Jonathan Brice.

"Carol Brice, Contralto Town Hall, March 30, 3:00," *Musical America,* 1 April 1952, 18

A large audience turned out to greet Carol Brice upon her return to Town Hall for her first New York appearance since 1949. Miss Brice opened with a Schubert group, and the agility with which she maneuvered her big rich voice in the delectable *Fischerweise* was an indication of the admirable vocal technique at her command. Turning to songs from Hugo Kauder's *Zwolf Gedichte* (in their first New York performance) the contralto sang with disarming simplicity and strikingly opulent chest tones. The songs themselves are somber and the piano accompaniment, exceptionally economical of material — even a bit bare, perhaps — was rather in the nature of an obligato to the flexible vocal line. A Bach group, to which incidental assistance by a string quartet and two flutes lent variety, brought the first half of the program to a close. The long, smooth phrases of "Esurientes Implevit" Bonis demonstrated most successfully the contralto's breath control and added immensely to the lilting charm of her delivery.

More new music opened the second half of the program, when Miss Brice sang Ernani Braga's settings of five delightful Brazilian folk tunes. These were perhaps the high points of her recital, for she summoned a wealth of color and a magnificent dramatic sense to aid her in her first-rate interpretations. A group in English was something of a letdown, mainly because the songs (barring Jean Berger's "Lonely People") were not particularly attractive. But in the closing group of Negro spirituals the contralto had sturdier material to work with, and the results were by turns amusing and touching.

If there were any blurs on the pattern of a most enchanting afternoon they were in Schubert's "Rastlose Liebe" and Bach's "Et Exultavit," in neither of which Miss Brice seemed able to retain the ringing resonance of her voice at the points of greatest intensity. Jonathan Brice, the singer's brother, was her sensitive accompanist.

"Carol Brice, Contralto Town Hall, Dec. 4, 2:30," *Musical America,* 15 December 1955, 22–23

Not that it should have come as a surprise to anyone, but from the very first notes of her latest recital it was evident that Carol Brice is a singer splendidly endowed by nature. Hers is a true contralto. Rather shaded in quality, the voice is nonetheless vibrant and clean; what is more, she uses it in a way that is remarkably true as to intonation and adept technically. While Miss Brice's high notes occasionally sound edgy and unfocused, the middle register is creamy and the lows are thrilling.

Vivaldi's "Stabat Mater," which opened the program, came across a bit inflexibly, but with the "Jubilate Domino" of Dietrich Buxtehude the singer had warmed up a supple and effective performance. Sheppard Coleman, playing the cello obligato, seconded her in a workmanlike manner. There followed a group of six songs by Hugo Wolf, which, in their fanciful but intense variety, shed light not only on Miss Brice's solid musicianship, but on her limitations as well. The most rewarding of these pieces, and possibly the best-sung offering of the afternoon, proved to be "Herr, was tragt der Boden hier?" delivered with long and lovely lines and a wealth of affecting interpretative detail. "Liebe mir im Busen zundet," on the other hand, betrayed a want of agility — but temperamental rather than technical. The difficulties of the music were bested, but one felt a certain lack of expressive rapport between the singer and the song.

The feeling was crystalized in the subsequent work, Beethoven's "Ah, Perfido!" This was simply too extensive in scope. Formalized posturizing, stirring though they may be in other hands, are not for an artist of such vital and transparent sincerity; Miss Brice was too true to herself to be successful in a mood of this sort.

Of six Christmas songs in various idioms, most moving was the unaccompanied "Po' Lil' Jesus," rich in depths of spiritual resource. "Four Preludes" by Irving Mopper, brief bits of deft calligraphy to poems of Langston Hughes, received a local premiere. The recital wound up with seasonable radiance in a setting of Psalm 150 by Louie White. At the piano throughout was the thoughtful and accomplished Jonathan Brice.

"Carol Brice to Town Hall," *New York Amsterdam News,* 25 January 1958, 7

The Inter-Branch Council of the National Association of College Women is presenting Carol Brice in concert at Town Hall on Friday, Feb. 7 at 8:30 p.m.

Miss Brice's brother, Jonathan, will accompany her.

Her program will consist of German, English, and Italian songs and a group of spirituals.

"Miss Brice Gives Delightful Concert," *New York Amsterdam News,* 15 February 1958, 13

Carol Brice, contralto, was presented by the National Association of College Women in a glowing and delightful concert last Friday evening at Town Hall. Despite the weather, an appreciative crowd gathered to hear this outstanding artist sing a program of selections in various languages.

Her rich and vibrant tone quality was brought out especially in "Nymphs and Shepherds" by Henry Purcell and in the German selection "Ich bin der Welt abhanden gekommen" by Gustav Mahler.

In a more fiery and dashing mood she sang "Trost im Ungluck"—a song about a German Calvaryman who has had enough of the foolishness of love.

Miss Brice's Italian was outstanding in the aria "Mura Felci," by Rossini. Here, smoothness and flexibility were demonstrated, "El Vito," from the Spanish, was lively and charming. She also sang a selection in Portuguese. This was done with a smooth lyric quality.

Lastly, she presented a rousing group of Spirituals to which she gave an interesting interpretation. She displayed volume, power and color in these songs, yet never sacrificing sweetness and melody. Mention the rich and excellent accompaniment of Jonathan Brice, her brother. He played the complete program from memory.

Miss Brice responded with several encores.

"Brice Debuts Next Week," *New York Amsterdam News,* 12 April 1958, 11

The Eastern Premiere of "The Ballad of Baby Doe" took place at the opening of the New York City Center's opera season last Thursday evening.

This Thursday "Lost in the Stars" will be presented with a preview Wednesday night and a cast, headed by Lawrence Winters and including such stars as Lee Charles, Nicholas Joy, Olga James, Rosetta LeNoire, Louis Gossett, Frederick O'Neal and Godfrey Cambridge.

"Lost in the Stars" will also be presented on April 20, 24, 25 and on May 3.

Next Thursday, April 17, Carol Brice makes her debut with the company in "Regina," with music and text by Marc Blitzstein.

"Carol Brice Is 'Saratoga' Hit," *New York Amsterdam News,* 23 January 1960, 15

"There is hardly anything one learns during her lifetime that doesn't stand her in good stead at one time or another."

This is the profound observation of world-famous contralto Carol Brice who is currently starring as Kakou in the hit Broadway musical "Saratoga."

Sitting in her second floor dressing room at the Winter Garden Theater, dreamy eyed and smiling, the lovely Miss Brice offered advice to youths which she regrets, she, herself did not follow.

"When aspiring to a musical career, study everywhere as earnestly as you can. Be prepared in all phases of the arts. Learn to act, dance as well as sing.

"Prepare yourself for opera as well as concertizing. If young people do this, there will come a day in their lives when they'll get on their knees and thank their Maker for having done so."

North Carolinian. Bent on a musical career since she could toddle, Miss Brice is grateful for the extensive dramatic training she received at Talladega College in Alabama and Palmer Memorial Institute in Sedalia, North Carolina.

When the "Saratoga" curtain goes up, the world-renowned contralto is on stage and remains on stage through two thirds of the show. Companion to Cleo, played by Carol Lawrence, it's Miss Brice's lines which set the tone and stage for things to come.

Bossy, yet lovable, she reminds the young southern white lady that her great grandmother came from the West Indies and was a Negro.

Besides her acting, Miss Brice gives the audience a fine emotional evening when, in her wonderful artistry, she sings two solos, "Getting a Man and Getting a Husband Are Two Different Things" and "Goose Never Be a Peacock."

The Broadway star has only one regret — she didn't study opera. Being a practical lady, this is why.

"I am a singer who never aspired to singing opera as a career because

I came along at a time when Roland Hayes, Paul Robeson and Marian Anderson were luminaries.

"At that time, opera was closed to Negroes and the doors of my mind were shut to entertaining opera as a career, even though I wanted to with all my heart."

Although Miss Brice thinks it's a bit late to begin studying opera from the ground up, weekly she attends two opera workshops and studies light roles to satisfy her hungry yearning to be an opera singer.

After having concertized throughout the world, she explains her crowning achievement will be returning to Europe and concertizing for the European people. Even though music lovers there are similar to those the world over, she pointed out, they are not inhibited and stand up, stomp, yell, scream, and just about get hoarse cheering your performances, she said.

"Miss Brice Sings Sun. at Coffee Concert," *New York Amsterdam News,* 23 January 1960, 13

Carol Brice, eminent contralto currently appearing in the Broadway show, "Saratoga," will be the featured artist in the third annual Winter Coffee Concert to be held Sunday evening, Jan. 24, in the Little Auditorium of St. Martin's Church, 230 Lenox Ave. at 122nd St. at 7:30 p.m.

Miss Brice will be accompanied at the piano by her brother Jonathan Brice. Other artists participating in the program of all Spanish music are John Carter, pianist, and Leonid Bolotine, guitarist.

Eugene Brice
(c. 1913–1980)

And of course, you know Eugene was her [Carol Brice's] brother. I knew him, too. He was doing a lot of singing in that whole period there. Bass-baritone, good voice. The other brother, Jonathan Brice, accompanied both of them. He was an excellent accompanist. One of the first top first-rate black accompanists in European literature.

— *William Warfield, April 21, 1994*

There are some that may be familiar with contralto Carol Brice. Her brother, Eugene, was not nearly as well known. He was a bass-baritone and toured with his sister and his brother, pianist Jonathan Brice, in the

Brice Family Trio. Eugene's credits also venture onto the concert stage and in opera, including Gershwin's *Porgy and Bess* and Marc Blitzstein's *Regina*. He died on Halloween of 1980 in New York City.

SOURCES

Obituary: *The Black Perspective in Music,* Vol. 9, No. 2, 239.

Anita Patti Brown
(c. 1870s or '80s–1950s)

In spite of her active career, very little is known of Anita Patti Brown's early life. She was born in Georgia, according to the press, and raised in Chattanooga, Tennessee. Her singing career began in an African Methodist Episcopal (AME) Church choir in Indianapolis, Indiana. Shortly after the turn of the century she settled in Chicago. In March of 1903 she appeared at the Chicago Opera House, her soprano debut. Due to her numerous appearances across the United States, the West Indies, and South America, she was dubbed "the globe-trotting prima donna" by the African American press of the day. She made her New York debut in Walter Craig's Pre-Lenten Recital in January of 1915. Tenor Roland Hayes and Helen Elise Smith (Mrs. R. Nathaniel Dett) were also featured on the program.

Brown toured with the "Black Devils," 370th Infantry Band, Eighth Illinois Regiment, after the First World War. George E. Dulf led the ensemble. She was also one of the first African American concert artists to make phonograph recordings. In 1916 she made records for the Victor Phonograph Company, and in 1920 for Black Swan Records. She studied voice in Europe during the 1920s and gave recitals there as well. In the 1930s she was back in Chicago and eventually taught voice privately. Her husband was Arthur Brown, one of the founders of the Umbrian Glee Club.

SOURCES

Cuney-Hare, Maud, *Negro Musicians and Their Music* (Washington, D.C.: Da Capo Press, 1936), 234.
Southern, Eileen, *Biographical Dictionary of Music and Musicians* (Westport, CT: Greenwood Press, 1982), 47.

Anne Wiggins Brown
(1915–)

Anne Wiggins Brown, yes of course, she was the first Bess ... The first time I saw *Porgy and Bess* I was a teenager and I was visiting some friends of mine from Corning, New York. They had relatives in New York [City], and that was a Saturday afternoon, and we decided we would go and look at Broadway. We looked up and there we saw *Porgy and Bess*. We had a little money in our pockets [so] we went in and saw *Porgy and Bess*. And I remember coming out. I was completely taken in. All of the street noises were like distant sounds. And it never dawned on me, when I saw [the production] and came out, that I would ever do [*Porgy and Bess*]. Neither did it dawn on me when I saw [Paul] Robeson that I'd ever do *Show Boat*.

By that time it was the production that Cheryl Crawford had done. The "Porgy" was done with the Theatre Guild and it was not a success. The Gershwins wanted it to be a thing at the Met and the Met was not going to use black singers then. As a matter of fact [the Met] had it all planned. The leads were to be Helen Jepson and Lawrence Tibbett. And one of the stipulations that Gershwin made was "No!" If it cannot be done with black artists, and especially a black chorus. They would not allow it to be done. And this is true even to this day. So, the Met wouldn't touch it because they were not hiring blacks at the Met at that time ... It really didn't take on Broadway the first time. Then a gal named Cheryl Crawford picked it up a couple of years later. And she brought it back to the format of what was the typical thing that was done on Broadway, which was dialogue interspersed with song ... She went back then and took the original dialogue from the DuBose Heywood play and made it run like a drama interspersed with songs. That's the version that I first saw. I didn't really see any version that brought it back to the full stature that was finally done at the Met, with all of the recitatives and all of that, until I did it myself in 1952. It was back during that time that I saw Anne Brown do it and met her ... She was a fabulous actress, a lovely voice, lyric soprano.

— *William Warfield, April 21, 1994*

In 1935 soprano Anne Wiggins Brown made history when she created the role of Bess in George Gershwin's opera *Porgy and Bess*. She received certificates in voice from the Institute of Musical Art in New York in 1932 and 1934. That institution is now known as the Juilliard

Portrait of Anne Wiggins Brown. Courtesy of the E. Azalia Hackley Collection, Detroit Public Library.

School of Music. While at the institute she studied with Licia Dunham. Brown also studied at Morgan College in Baltimore, Maryland, and at Columbia University Teachers College in New York.

Throughout the 1930s she sang on Broadway in many musicals, including *Mamba's Daughters* in 1939 and *La Belle Helene*, also in 1939.

She returned to the role of Bess in a 1942 revival of *Porgy and Bess*. European productions of Gershwin's opera were soon to follow; among them were performances in Sweden in 1947 and 1948. In 1950 Brown starred in Menotti's *The Medium* and *The Telephone* in Norway.

From 1942 to 1948 she toured throughout the United States and Canada, adding Europe to her schedule in 1946. In addition to giving recitals and appearances with symphony orchestras, she also appeared on television programs. She settled in Norway in 1948, continuing her concert career and teaching voice to young singers.

SOURCES

Cuney-Hare, Maud, *Negro Musicians and Their Music* (Washington, D.C.: Da Capo Press, 1936), 263.
Southern, Eileen, *Biographical Dictionary of Afro-American and African Musicians* (Westport, CT: Greenwood Press, 1982), 50.

"Guest Star," *New York Amsterdam News,* 22 July 1939, 17

Anne Wiggins Brown, soprano who appeared with Todd Duncan, the Eva Jessye Choir and Oscar Levant as guest star with Alexander Smallens, the conductor, at the second annual George Gershwin memorial program at Lewisohn Stadium Monday before a capacity audience.

"Soprano in Motherhood Role," *New York Amsterdam News,* 28 October 1939, 12

There's a daughter in the family of Dr. and Mrs. C.C. (Jack) Pettit, of 1864 Seventh Avenue. Born late Tuesday night, October 17, at Hudson View Hospital, she and her mother were doing nicely at press time. Who knows but what the little miss chirps in a lovely lyric soprano voice? She weighed six pounds eleven and three quarter ounces at birth.

The Pettits were married here May 7 of last year, Mrs. Pettit being the famous soprano, Anne Wiggins Brown, formerly of Baltimore. A graduate of the Institute of Musical Art of the Juilliard Foundation, Mrs. Pettit played the role of Bess in George Gershwin's operatic version of "Porgy and Bess" and Lissa in Dubose and Dorothy Heyward's "Mamba's Daughters" which also starred Ethel Waters and Georgette Harvey in its successful Broadway show closed in the summer, because of this anticipated "Blessed Event," and Mrs. Pettit did not rejoin the cast for its current road run. The baby's father is a well-known chiropodist and aviator.

Thelma Waide Brown
(1897–1975)

Thelma Waide Brown was one of the most highly respected African American concert singers and teachers in the Chicago area for many years. Born in 1897, she toured as a concert singer and also sang in numerous opera productions. Numbered among her most notable productions were *Aida*, *Samson and Delilah*, and *Messiah*, which she performed in Chicago. For more than twenty-six years Brown taught at Chicago's Roosevelt College. She received awards from the National Association of Business Women and the National Association of Negro Musicians. Thelma Brown died on August 25, 1975, in Chicago.

SOURCES

Obituary: *The Black Perspective in Music*, Vol. 4, No. 3, 344.

William Brown

Renowned for his technical virtuosity, beautiful tone, and interpretive commitment (*The Boston Globe*), internationally acclaimed concert, opera and recording artist William Brown commands a repertoire encompassing practically all musical genres. The tenor has performed with orchestras throughout the world, including the Royal Philharmonic, London Symphony, Orquesta Filarmonica, Helsinki Philharmonic, Czech National Symphony, the New York Philharmonic, and Cleveland and Boston Symphonies. His operatic engagements include the New York City Opera, Baltimore, Florentine, Opera South and Ebony Opera. He has appeared on all of the major U. S. Television networks and the CBC Network in Canada. His recordings include CBS Records, London, Nonesuch, New World, Telarc, CRI, Gun Mar, and Musical Heritage Records. *Ebony* magazine listed Mr. Brown as one of the "ten new voices of the eighties," and the state of Mississippi honored him with a William Brown Day. An avid performer of Twentieth Century music, he has appeared with many major contemporary music ensembles and has been honored with several compositions written especially for him. He is a charter member of the

Black Music Research Ensemble, Chicago, Illinois, and he holds an honorary doctorate from Bridgewater College, Massachusetts.

"Fi-Yer! A Century of African American Song," *Society for American Music Bulletin,* **Volume XXVI, No. 1, Spring 2000**

> *FI-YER! A Century of African American Song.* (William Brown, tenor; Ann Sears, piano. Albany Records, Troy 329, 1999. One compact disc.)
> ...The genius of these fresh performances is a combination of the daring and imaginative with the careful and calculated. Brown has found a great foil here in the finesse and clarity of Sears' piano accompaniments, which are no less assertive and confident than the principal voice. Brown's stylized range of vocal moves includes scoops, slides, blue notes, and a whole palette of timbral shadings—a beguilingly whole mosaic of gestures. Because he has adopted his formidable vocal technique to the rhetorical demands of the culture, *Fi-Yer!* elucidates the expressive interrelations between field, street, and concert hall in African American heritage.
>
> —William T. Dargan, *St. Augustine's College*

Grace Bumbry
(1937–)

Grace Melzia Ann Bumbry was born in St. Louis, Missouri, on January 4, 1937. Like her contemporary Shirley Verrett, she began her singing career as a mezzo-soprano and later added soprano roles. She studied at Boston University and Northwestern University. She also studied with Lotte Lehmann at the Music Academy of the West in Santa Barbara (1955–1958) and with Pierre Bernac in Paris. In 1958 she and Martina Arroyo were co-winners of the Metropolitan Opera auditions. Two years later she had a successful debut with the Paris Opera in the role of Amneris. The following year she made history by being the first African American artist to appear at the Bayreuth Festival singing the role of Venus in Wagner's *Tannhäuser.* Debuts at other major opera companies soon followed. Bumbry debuted at Covent Garden and the Chicago Lyric Opera in 1963, the Metropolitan Opera in 1965, the Vienna Staatsoper in 1966, La Scala in 1974 and appeared in Salzburg in 1964. Her most distinguished roles include Carmen, Salome, Delilah, Tosca, Eboli, Lady Macbeth, Azucena and Fricka. In 1985 she sang the role of Bess for the premiere of *Porgy and Bess* at the Metropolitan Opera. At the opening of the Bastile Opera in Paris in 1990 she sang Cassandra in Berlioz's *Prise de Troie*.

SOURCES

Abdul, Raoul, *Blacks in Classical Music: A Personal History* (New York: Dodd, Mead, 1978).
Blyth, Alan, "Grace Bumbry," *Opera xxi*, 1970, 506–510.
Hitchcock, H. Wiley, and Stanley Sadie, eds., *The New Grove Dictionary of American Music* (London: Macmillan, 1986).

Rosa Louise Burge
(1908–1986)

Many people felt that Louise Burge, who came right along during the time of Marian Anderson, would've been equally well known if Marian Anderson had not been the reigning person. But that was back in those days when there was one of us doing everything, you know. *A* Marian Anderson, *a* Roland Hayes, *a* Paul Robeson, *a* William Warfield later who's going to be *a* Paul Robeson. It was all like that. And Louise Burge herself was a consummate artist ... I think the thing that was the big difference, in what I had heard explained to me, was hers was a deeper contralto sound as such. Marian Anderson had sort of like a double voice. She could do the mezzo stuff, like in *Ave Maria* [by Franz Schubert], then she could go down and do *Trampin'*, an octave lower, and sound like a man. But the true classification of contralto which blends, say, from a G down to another G, they say Louise Burge was. A very rich sound ... Unfortunately, by the time I met her, she was older and was not singing anymore. I think she was still teaching at Howard [University] at the time and I got to meet her ... A lady of stature in every way. I was just totally impressed with her and said, "Oh gosh! I'd love to hear her sing."

— *William Warfield, April 21, 1994*

A native of Kay Spring, Georgia, contralto Rosa Louise Burge was born on July 9, 1908. While still in high school she toured with the Knoxville College Sextet of Tennessee and later attended Knoxville College Academy. Joining the student body at Howard University, in 1929, she studied voice with Lulu V. Childers and eventually earned two baccalaureate degrees from that institution. She also earned a master's degree from the Teachers College of Columbia University. Burge obtained a great deal of additional vocal study from the Juilliard School and in England, France, Italy, and Germany.

For four years she taught at A & M State College at Pine Bluff, Arkansas. In 1942 she joined the voice faculty of Howard University and became the assistant director of the University Choir. She retired from the performing arena in 1976 and joined the voice faculty of Trinity College. The Music Department of Howard University in 1982, for her years of service and dedication, paid a public tribute to Burge. She died on July 9, 1986, in Washington, D.C.

SOURCES

McGinty, Doris E., *The Black Perspective in Music,* Vol. 14, No. 3, 323.

New York Amsterdam News, 6 July 1940, 11 (originally beneath a photo)

> Thirteen thousand music lovers were at the Lewisohn Stadium on Tuesday night, June 25 when Louise Burge, brilliant contralto (shown at the top right with flowers), sang the solo section of the new Chapin-Still ballad poem for chorus, *And They Lynched Him on a Tree.* Katherine Garrison Chapin, the poet, is pictured with Miss Burge.

Harry (Henry) Thacker Burleigh
(1866–1949)

Harry (Henry) Thacker Burleigh was born in Erie, Pennsylvania, on December 2, 1866. His mother possessed a college degree and spoke fluent French and Greek. However, unable to secure a position due to her race, she worked as a domestic. The need to achieve a solid education came from his mother's influence. His grandfather, Hamilton Waters, was his first major musical influence. Mr. Waters was a town crier and lamplighter for Erie. He often sang plantation songs for his grandson, who would one day become the most respected African American musician and artist of his day and who would in turn influence generations of artists.

Harry attended the National Conservatory of Music in New York in

1892, where he received a scholarship. While at the conservatory he studied voice with Fritsch, harmony with Goldmark and counterpoint with White and Spicker. While a student he befriended Edward MacDowell, Victor Herbert and his biggest influence to date, Antonin Dvorak.

Burleigh sang numerous spirituals for Dvorak, who in turn used "Swing Low, Sweet Chariot" and the spiritual idiom as a basis for his Symphony no. 9, "For the New World." Burleigh and Sissieretta Jones were the featured soloists at New York's Madison Square Garden for Dvorak's arrangement of "Old Folks at Home." In 1894 Burleigh became the baritone soloist for New York's prestigious St. George's Episcopal Church choir. He was the first African American to hold the position. He would also become the first African American to serve as soloist for Temple Emanu-El, a New York synagogue.

Throughout his career Burleigh became a powerful force and treasured influence among African Americans, and eventually America at-large, as a baritone recitalist, pianist, composer and lecturer. His 1916 piano-vocal arrangement of "Deep River" was the first spiritual to be written in art song form. It would set the standard for future generations of composers of spiritual arrangements. Over the years Burleigh performed for the Queen of England and President Theodore Roosevelt. He championed the careers of Marian Anderson, Paul Robeson, William Grant Still, Margaret Bonds, Dorothy Maynor and Carol Brice. He was a charter member of the American Society of Composers, Authors and Publishers (ASCAP) at its founding in 1914, and became a mem-

Portrait of Harry T. Burleigh, May 1916. Photographs and Prints Division, Schomburg Center for Research in Black Culture, The New York Public Library, Astor, Lenox and Tilden Foundations.

ber of its board in 1941. He received honorary degrees from Atlanta University and Howard University, and was awarded the Spingarn Medal. He died on September 12, 1948, of heart failure in Stamford, Connecticut. He was 82. The pallbearers at his funeral included Hall Johnson, Eubie Blake, William C. Handy and Cameron White.

SOURCES

Abdul, Raoul, *Blacks in Classical Music: A Personal History* (New York: Dodd, Mead, 1978).

Kramer, A. Walter, "H. T. Burleigh: Composer by Divine Right and the American Coleridge-Taylor," *Musical America*, 29 April 1916, 25.

Simpson, Anne Key, *Hard Trials: the Life and Music of Harry T. Burleigh* (New Jersey: Scarecrow Press, 1990).

"Deep River" Popularizes a Composer, *Boston Evening Transcript*, 10 March 1917

Those who have heard concerts during the present season have probably noticed on the programs one song more than any other. This is "Deep River," credited to Harry T. Burleigh. Although this song is only Mr. Burleigh's arrangement of a famous old Negro "spiritual" it has justly brought him into prominence which he has long deserved. His songs have for two or three seasons past been sung by a list of prominent singers which would make any composer's mouth water. Recently, according to reports, which have come from across the ocean, his song, "The Young Warrior," has gained great popularity in Italy as a sort of patriotic anthem of the present war. With orchestration provided by Zandonai it has been widely sung in concert.

These two pieces, fine as they are, only introduce the excellent body of work which Mr. Burleigh has accomplished in the past five or six years. Altogether Ricordi & Company, Mr. Burleigh's publishers, have issued some three dozen of his songs. In them one notices a marked facility in the invention of melody, an unusual cleverness in the construction of rich yet clear accompaniment, and marked power of musical articulation. Indeed the "Five Songs of Laurence Hope" must be regarded as among the very best which have recently been produced in America. The popular qualities of this music are evident in the first hearing. One can easily understand that the melting tones of John McCormack's voice have made thousands applaud them. But it is not so evident, until one comes to study them, how much musicianship and taste have gone into their construction.

Mr. Burleigh modestly insists that he is not a composer. It is his way of saying that composition has necessarily been little more than a luxury with him. He has been subject to the grind of the poor musician. He has been forced to earn his living as a singer as baritone soloist at St. George's Church, at the Temple Emanu-El in New York, and as the efficient executant of all those little odd jobs that fall to the lot of the conscientious musician who must keep body and soul together as best he can. Mr. Burleigh was the son of two Negro servants in the house of a rich woman of Erie, Pennsylvania. As a little boy he hung around the music rooms when eminent visitors came to play, and early he became conscious of the fact that somehow, someway, he would be a musician. When friends made it possible, he came to New York in 1892 and through the interest of Mrs. MacDowell, mother of the composer, obtained a scholarship in the National Conservatory of Music, then under the direction of Anton Dvorak. Here after studying singing, harmony and counterpoint, he became an instructor, and presently established himself in New York as a baritone soloist. It was only some eight or ten years ago, long after his graduation from the conservatory that the possibility of composition occurred to him.

The small group of songs by which Mr. Burleigh is best known include "Deep River," "The Grey Wolf," "Ethiopia Saluting the Colors," "The Young Warrior," "The Soldier," and "Jean." The rune-like two-line melody of "Deep River" was Coleridge-Taylor's favorite "spiritual," and Mr. Burleigh was farvisioned enough to appreciate its availability for the concert hall. Supplying a very simple middle section, he built the tune into a song as compactly organized as one of Schubert's. The moving climax is hardly surpassed in emotional intensity in many a renowned song. Mr. Burleigh's accompaniment, however, is neither difficult nor unusual. It makes no attempt at exotic or racial effect. For Mr. Burleigh has little faith in the availability of negro tones as accompaniments for a special style or "School" of music. Although he has interested himself to the extent of making choral arrangements of some of the "spirituals," no one in studying the songs would guess the composer's race. Some may wish that "Deep River" had been arranged with a view to carrying out the negro elements of the melody, but none could ask for a more effective piece for the concert hall.

"The Young Warrior" was composed shortly after the opening of the present war to words by James Weldon Johnson, who was minister to Nicaragua under President Roosevelt. The lyric is the appeal of the young volunteer to his mother to think not of him but of the work he is to do. Mr. Burleigh has given the words one of those melodies that sing themselves—not exalted in style, but ruddy with the enthusiasm of the mob in this its patriotic frenzy. Beneath this melody is an accompaniment composed of trumpet calls and crashing chords. Probably Mr. Burleigh himself would not claim high artistic excellence for this song, but it has that quality of mob enthusiasm, which few of the highly trained composers can manage.

"The Grey Wolf" to words of Arthur Symons is a long declamatory scena designed for a robust dramatic voice. The heroic mood of this piece is all too rarely cultivated in present-day composition. The voice part is written with sensitive regard for the dramatic values of the words, and the accompaniment, with its constantly shifting harmonic scheme, well expresses the emotional surge underneath. More notable than the actual musical content is the composer's feeling for structural effect. Here one finds one of his most typical devices, the repeated use of brief dramatic snatches — now entwined in the polyphonic structure and again dominant in the treble — toward a culminating emotional effect.

In "The Soldier" the use of thematic snatches is less artistic, being chiefly confined to quotations from English popular songs. But it is highly effective and is by no means without artistry in its management. The words are those of Rupert Brooke's now famous sonnet — "If I should die, think only this of me." It is a song of a soldier about to die, and the tramp of the funeral march is never long absent from its accompaniment. "Rule Britannia," the "British Grenadiers," and the English national anthem appear now and again in the voice part of the accompaniment. But more effective still is the brief theme of four notes, which is Mr. Burleigh's own. Here again, though the musical material lacks the final mark of distinction, the structure is so canny and well artificed that the song must be regarded as an able achievement.

Of the more ambitious songs, "Ethiopia Saluting the Colors" is certainly the best. The very choice of Walt Whitman's words for musical setting indicates the serious and ambitious quality of the composer's musical instinct. The poem is a brief ballad of Sherman's march to the sea. The Union soldier sees an old Negro woman looking out from the doorway of her hovel and curtsying to the regiments. The half-witted hag understands nothing of the mighty drama that is being enacted for her sake, but the soldier catches glimpses of the epic in which he is an actor — that of the peaceful farmer called from his mowing to right the ancient wrong of two continents. The music moves upon the discordant tread of the marching army. A barbaric melody calls to mind the dark continent whence it and "Ethiopia" were both fetched over sea, and now and then the opening phrase of "Marching through Georgia" enters to give life to the picture. The scene is moving tableaux, ably depicted, and admirably suited to the declamatory talent of a singer like Mr. Witherspoon, who has sung it and to whom it is dedicated. One wishes that American song literature contained a greater proportion of such extended pieces, which combine the dramatic with the lyric, and offer much more for the listener to get hold of than is afforded by brief jets of song.

The "Five Songs of Laurence Hope" probably represent Mr. Burleigh's best work. Here are haunting melodies, accompaniments rich in detail, yet not overwritten, striking bits of delineation, and much skill in the wedding of music to words. In sheer emotional effectiveness these songs must receive high rank. Once more the composer shows much cleverness in the weaving of brief thematic snatches into the harmonic framework. The second song of the group, "The Jungle Flower," gains distinction from the exotic pulsating syncopation that throbs beneath. The third, "Pale Hands I Lov'd," is perhaps the best achieved of the five. Here the moody sentiment of the words is heightened into something approaching tragic pathos. In the fourth song, "Among the Fuchias," Mr. Burleigh has caught admirably that oriental exoticism which is none the less charming because it happens to be fashionable in present day song literature. The final song, "Till I Wake," is a lyric of real distinction. The impressive opening theme is intoned as though by brass choir, giving way to its statement by the voice above an accompaniment of wide arpeggi. Later this theme reaches a passionate climax introducing the words, "If there be an awakening," and the song ends in an emotional lyric strain. Though Mr. Burleigh has taken pains in these pieces, as in all his songs, to give the text its full value, he writes in melodic rather than a declamatory idiom. The chief characteristic of the accompaniments beyond their clever use of themes, is their easy chromatic flow.

The remaining songs are more nearly of the conventional type of "light concert pieces," which are beloved of singers for the latter part of their programs. As such they are notably successful and reveal invention and musicianship well above the average. The four songs grouped under the general title Passionale (words by James Weldon Johnson) offer grateful material to the accomplished tenor. Best of them is "The Glory of the Day Was in Her Face," which is at once suave and impassioned. "In the Wood of Finvara" is admirable in its creation of atmosphere by simple means. Even better of the sort is "By the Pool at the Third Rosses," to words by Arthur Symons. "The Prayer" is a simple melody set over a hymn-like accompaniment, well constructed and modulated. "The Hour Glass" has certain dignified sentimentality, with its chorale-like theme and its quotation from the Dresden liturgy. "Memory," in spite of its conventional strain, is not without distinction. "Three Shadows," sung by John McCormack, is a frankly sentimental and wholly delightful bit of melody, which well deserves its popularity.

The Southland Sketches are four pieces for violin and piano, based on Negro themes. Yet they are in no sense an attempt to set in relief the Negroid musical characteristics. Rather, they are aimed and well fashioned for practical effectiveness in the authorized manner. The Andante, a wistful and ingratiating piece, preserved just a trace of the rhythmic sparkle of the Negro tune. The Allegretto Graziono, strongly recalling Dvorak's "Humoresque," is altogether charming, and the final allegro is brimming with high spirit.

In nearly all of Mr. Burleigh's work we recognize the earnest and talented musician. His choice of texts for his songs indicates a refinement of taste which is revealed again in his selection and moulding of his best themes. The robust spirit that dictated "Ethiopia Saluting the Colors" is one that is much needed to lift American song literature from the deadly average of mediocrity which now holds it fast. Better things can be expected of Mr. Burleigh than those, which he has thus far done. He has visibly grown in musical stature in the last five years, the later songs being so much better in workmanship than the earlier ones that they seem the result of a hew inspiration. If he persists in the mood of his more ambitious undertakings he may prove a force as stimulating to musical composition as he has been charming to concert audiences.

"Harry T. Burleigh Honored Today at St. George's," reprinted from the clipping file at the Schomberg Library (New York), 30 March 1925 (source of clipping unknown)

Fashionable St. George's Church, among whose communicants are numbered the J. Pierpont Morgans and Knickerbocker families of national and international prominence, is today paying an unusual tribute to Harry T. Burleigh, Negro singer and composer, in recognition of his thirty years service as baritone soloist in the choir.

A special music program is being held in the church this afternoon at 4 o'clock. All the numbers sung by the vested choir of some eighty white singers are Negro spirituals arranged by Mr. Burleigh.

The program has been in course of preparation for weeks. George W. Kemmer, organist and choirmaster, sent out hundreds of postal cards on which was printed the order of music, which follows:

Processional 495; "Nobody Knows the Trouble I've Seen;" "Weeping Mary;" violin solo: "Southland Sketches 111;" "My Lord, What a Mornin';" vesper hymn, "I Hope My Mother Will Be There;" "The Reiland Amen;" and recessional, "Let Us Cheer the Weary Traveler."

Special Leaflet Printed. At the instance of the Rev. Karl Reiland, rector, a special form of leaflet was printed for this afternoon's service. On it are two pictures of the singer — one as he looked thirty years ago and the other as he appears today. The introductory reading on the leaflet proclaims "the thirtieth anniversary of Harry T. Burleigh's membership as baritone soloist of St. George's Church." An interesting sketch of Burleigh's active life also was printed for free distribution.

It is Burleigh's boast that throughout the thirty years of his association with St. George's choir he has not missed a Sunday, except in the course of his vacations. On one occasion he was unavoidably detained in the morning, but was present at the other services. When his mother died he went to Erie, PA, to attend her funeral, returning the next day and participating in the musical program.

Many Hard Knocks. Harry T. Burleigh's career has been a medley of hard knocks, hard work, and the ultimate attainment of just recognition. He played for years up and down the scale of adversity before finding himself in time and in tune with success.

Inherently a musician, born with a singing voice of promise and an unquenchable ambition to be somebody in the realm of music, he was brought face to face at an early age with two handicaps—poverty and race prejudice.

His mother, whom he calls his inspiration and guiding spirit, was a college graduate who spoke French fluently. When unmarried she had applied for a position as teacher in the public schools, but race prejudice was so rife at the time she was unsuccessful. Later on, a widow, she became janitress of the school where she had aspired to be a teacher.

"My mother was a singer and I remember when a lad how she used to sing as she went about cleaning P.S. No. 1 of Erie. My father, Reginald, and I would indulge in a bit of harmonizing as we dusted the desks and helped mother all we could," declared Mr. Burleigh, reverting to the earliest of his innumerable struggles.

"I don't recall when I started singing, it seems I have been doing so since infancy. I was about twelve years old when my brother and I got the job of lighting the street lamps in the 1st ward of Erie. They were oil lamps and we had to use matches. I found a lot of solace in singing as I started out to extinguish the lamps at 4 o'clock in the morning. A few hours later would find me delivering the Erie Dispatch to subscribers and still singing—possibly not as loudly as at daybreak.

"Even at an early age I was fired with a burning desire to hear all the musical artists that came to Erie. I never shall forget the time a company of singers headed by Campanini made their appearance at the Park Opera House. I was then running an elevator at the Reed House. Forgetting that the concert was to be presented in the evening, I managed to get by attaches of the theatre and make my way to the peanut gallery where I hid all afternoon between the benches. I did not stir, so fearful was I of detection. But I heard Campanini and his fellow artists and enjoyed the concert immensely."

Worked on Lake Steamers. Before coming to New York to take up the study of music Burleigh worked on lake steamers out of Buffalo as pantry-man and did various kinds of menial labor to keep the wolf from the door and help support his mother. When he abandoned his hometown for New York he had won some local recognition as a singer; having been a member of the choirs of St. Paul's Church, Park Presbyterian Church and the Jewish synagogue.

During the first years of Burleigh's stay in the metropolis as a musical student, he plumbed the depths of poverty. Often he went hungry for days. "I used to stand hungry in front of one of Dennett's downstairs restaurants and watch the man in the window cook cakes. Then I would take a toothpick from my pocket, use it as if I had eaten, draw on my imagination and walk down the street singing to myself. That happened more than once or twice."

Burleigh's Erie associations served him in good stead when he came to New York to win a scholarship in the National Conservatory of Music founded by Jeanette M. Thurber. Of this phase of his career the singer says: "At one of the concerts given at the Russell home Teresa Carreno was the visiting artist. In those days she was making her early American tours. I opened the door for her. I saw nothing more of her until 1892, when I came to New York.

"In taking examinations for a scholarship in the National Conserva-tory of Music, I entered the lists in voice. At the time, Dvorak was direc-tor of the conservatory. The late Joseffy Romualso Sapio and Adele Margulies were among the artists of renown on the jury. I think I was given ABA for reading and B for voice. I was told that AA was the required mark, below which I had fallen a little."

Wins a Scholarship. "The registrar happened to be a woman who had trav-eled with Carreno. When I learned from her of my failure I told her my cherished longings, and she sympathized with me. During our conversation she learned I came form Erie. I took a letter of recommendation from Mrs. Russell from my pocket and told her I was the boy who some years ago had opened the door when Mme. Carreno played at Mrs. Russell's.

"I was told to come back within a few days. When I did I was awarded a scholarship. The woman who befriended me was the mother of Edward MacDowell, famous composer. At the conservatory I helped Mrs. Mac-Dowell with the writing of class books, addressing letters and sending out circulars. I studied voice with Christian Fritsch, harmony with Rubin Goldmark, counterpoint with John White and Max Spicker. Later I played double bass and subsequently tympani in the Conservatory Orchestra under Frank Van der Stucken and Gustav Heinrichs and was librarian of the Orchestra."

The opinion prevailed in musical circles that Burleigh's contact with Anton Dvorak influenced the latter to compose the "New World Symphony." "Dvorak knew the tunes of our Negro spirituals," says Burleigh, "and he was familiar with 'Swing Low, Sweet Chariot' which the second theme of his first movement resembles strongly. I remember asking him one day which movement of this symphony he liked the best. He replied: 'I love them all alike; are they not all my children?' I used to play and sing these songs for him and he was keenly interested in them."

Thirty years ago, with sixty applicants competing, Burleigh won the position of baritone soloist at St. George's Church. The Rev. Dr. Rainsford was rector. "I can easily recall my feeling of timidity when I applied for a position in the choir," said Burleigh. "An usher told me I might get a chance to see Dr. Rainsford if I would hang around after services.' I remember my anxiety as I approached the man whose words, heard but a few moments before, had seemed so helpful and sincere."

Touched by the Honor. "I summoned courage and handed Dr. Rainsford my card. Reading it, he grasped my hand warmly and told me he would tell his organist of my application. Something in his tone and simple manner set me completely at ease. I left the church full of hope that a man who could be so big and yet so simple would not allow my color to prejudice him, but would give me a chance. I was the only Negro who applied and the position went to me. It has indeed been a rare privilege to be allowed to serve the good people of St. George's Church for so long a time. I am profoundly touched by the honor they are conferring upon me."

But for Burleigh's mother he would have given up singing in church choirs to become a musical director for Williams & Walker. In 1898 the two famous Negro comedians were starring in a musical show known as "The Senegambian Carnival." While at Koster & Bials, Burleigh was induced to go into the orchestra pit because of an emergency. So well did he acquit himself that the comedians made him a flattering offer to continue as their musical director. Acting on the advice of his mother, who advised him that the move would be unwise, he turned down with thanks the proposal to earn what was then considered a big salary.

It has devolved on Harry Burleigh to officiate as soloist at the homes of some of New York's distinguished citizens. At the request of the late J. Pierpont Morgan he sang "Calvary" at the financier's funeral. He also sang solos at the funerals of Seth Low and Henry Bacon, and he was in the choir at services held for the late Frank I. Cobb, editor of *The World*. But singing of Burleigh is not enjoyed exclusively by the rich and influential. Many poor people on the east side have been charmed and comforted by the baritone while on one of his missions of good cheer.

Burleigh has sung for Prince Henry of Prussia, Theodore Roosevelt, the Archbishop of Canterbury, Paderewski, Mme. Terina, Anton Seidl and other celebrities. He has not forgotten when he first sang for Victor Herbert at Saratoga, when the bandmaster and composer was assistant conductor of the Grand Union Hotel orchestra and Burleigh was a wine boy. "Victor Herbert never could get his wine cold enough those days," Burleigh asserts. The two musicians are friends to this day.

Wrote 250 Songs. Since becoming a composer Burleigh has written some 250 songs, several festival anthems and compositions for violin. In recent years he has won distinction for his arrangements of Negro spirituals.

"In what do you take more pride — being a singer, or composer?" Burleigh was asked. "I hope to make my greatest reputation as an arranger of Negro spirituals," he answered. "In Negro spirituals my race has pure gold, and they should be taken as the Negro's contribution to artistic possessions. In them we show a spiritual security as old as the ages. These songs always denote a personal relationship. It is my Savior, my sorrow, my kingdom. The personal note is ever present. America's only original and distinctive style of music is destined to be appreciated more and more."

Harry T. Burleigh was born in 1866. His physical appearance and mental vigor suggest a much younger man. There is no parallel for the conspicuous place he has made for himself in musical America and he is on the way to setting up a new record, for on April 1, 1925, he will celebrate his twenty-fifth anniversary as a baritone singer in the choir of the Temple Emanu-El.

"Swing Low, Sweet Chariot," *Coronet,* July 1947

Like his indestructible baritone, Burleigh's songs ignore the years and the fluctuations of the Hit Parade. Mocked once because he wanted to sing old songs, he now stands recognized as one of the foremost musical pioneers of his people. Wherever folks heed God and own a piano, you will hear his arrangements of America's well-loved spirituals.

"It's a wonderful thing," Burleigh says happily, "to feel that you amount to something in music."

His happiness and enthusiasm are infectious. When he talks about his mother, who spurred him to success, about his close friends of years ago — Victor Herbert, Anton Dvorak, John McCormack — his voice deepens with love. They are wonderful people, happy people, he recalls.

And when he speaks of his many protégés, Paul Robeson, Marian Anderson, Roland Hayes among them, his voice quickens with enthusiasm. Through the genius of such people, he hopes his race will some day reach the end of the long dark road of discrimination.

Harry Burleigh has walked that road himself. Hardships blinded his slave grandfather; discrimination frustrated his mother's career. Yet he is not bitter. "We've all gone through those things," he remarks quietly.

"To Be a Big Musical Event," *The New York Age*, 25 April 1912, 5

As will be seen by reference to the advertising columns of *The Age*, there is to be a great event for the colored people of New York on May 2, when a grand concert will be given at Carnegie Hall under the auspices and in aid of the recently formed Music School Settlement for the Colored People. This concert will be given exclusively by colored artists, who will sing and play compositions composed by colored musicians.

...The always-popular baritone, Harry T. Burleigh, will sing several songs.

...The Music School Settlement for Colored People has recently been incorporated under the laws of the State of New York, with a board of directors consisting of the following well known people: Elbridge L. Adams, Mrs. Frances C. Barlow, the Rev. Hutchins C. Bishop, Henry T. Burleigh, Miss Natalie Curtis, Miss Dorothea Draper, Dr. W. E. Burghardt Du Bois, Mrs. Benj. Guiness, the Rev. Wm. P. Hayes, Mrs. David Mannes, David Mannes, Mrs. W. H. McElroy, Winthrop L. Rogers, Mrs. Charles Sprague-Smith, Lyman Beecher Stowe, Frederick Strauss, Princess Pierre Troubetzkoy, Miss Louis Veltin and Miss Elizabeth Walton.

"Negroes Perform Their Own Music: Annual Concert Reveals but Little Interest in Serious Composition," *Musical America*, 21 March 1914, 37

Under the auspices and for the benefit of the Music School Settlement for Colored People in New York a concert was given at Carnegie Hall on March 11, made up of compositions by Negro musicians and interpreted by them.

The spirituals "Deep River" and "Dig My Grave," arranged by Harry T. Burleigh and conducted by him, were among the best things heard. Mr. Burleigh also sang, accompanying himself at the piano, his harmonizations of "You May Bury Me," "Weepin' Mary" and "I Don't Feel No-Ways Tired." He again proved himself an able musician.

...What is called the Negro Symphony Orchestra played two fine arrangements of Mr. Burleigh's (fine enough for our Philharminic or Symphony Orchestras to perform), compositions by James Reese Europe, Coleridge-Taylor, William H. Tyers, Will H. Dixon and E. E. Thompson.

...This concert, the third effort of those who wish to assert his musical individuality, though more creditable than the two previous, fell short once more of the serious purpose which these talents might be directed. Mr. Burleigh, for example, excellent musician that he is, after distinguishing himself by singing his spirituals, spoiled his contribution to the musical excellence of the program by singing the popular "Why Adam Sinned."

...It is to be granted that it will take some time to imbue these Negro musicians with a thorough musical appreciation, to teach them the difference between serious music and popular "song and dance" music. There is little excuse, however, for so many songs of an obvious "vaudeville" character being heard at a concert of this kind, and what is more being sung in the manner of the variety theaters. The northern Negro has neither the love nor the knowledge of what the old spirituals mean; and he does not sing them with warmth. This is Negro music however and it should be preserved.

Mayme Calloway-Byron

Mayme Calloway-Byron was said to have possessed a dramatic soprano voice of great range and power. The bulk of her work took place in Europe, the result being that she was little known in the United States. While in Europe she appeared with the Munich and Dresden Philharmonic Orchestras. When she returned to the United States, around the time of World War I, she settled in Chicago, Illinois. Engagements on the Pacific Coast were soon to follow.

SOURCES

Cuney-Hare, Maud, *Negro Musicians and Their Music* (Washington, D.C.: Da Capo Press, 1936), 234.

Minto Cato
(1900–1979)

Mezzo-soprano Minto Cato was born on September 4, 1900, in Little Rock, Arkansas. At Harriet Gibbs Marshal's Conservatory of Music, in Washington, D.C., she received her musical education. Her husband was the performer Joe Sheftal. During the early years of her career Cato toured with her husband's show, *Joe Sheftal and his Southland Revue*. On Broadway she sang in such musicals as *Keep Shufflin'* (1928), *Hot Chocolates* (1929), and *Blackbirds of 1930.* The opera world commanded her attention during the 1930s and '40s. She sang leading roles with Salmaggi's opera company and Mary Cardwell Dawson's National Negro Opera Company. Her most popular roles were in Verdi's *Aida, Il Trovatore,* and *La Traviata.*

SOURCES

Obituary: *The Black Perspective in Music,* Vol. 8, No. 2, 263.

New York Amsterdam News, 9 September 1939, 17

Minto Cato and Dick Hough threw a party Saturday nite that literally put Arkansas on the map (as if it weren't already 'cause we were born there) .... With her grand songs at the piano, Minto is without a doubt, Harlem's most entertaining hostess.

Estelle Pinckney Clough
(c. 1860/'70s—19?)

Estelle Pinckney Clough, soprano, was born in Worcester, Massachusetts, and probably died in the same area. She began her singing career in the 1880s giving concerts in Worcester and Boston, Massachusetts. During the 1890s she appeared in concerts in New York and along the East Coast. In 1903 her first major break came when she sang the title role in Verdi's *Aida* in Theodore Drury's New York production. When England's renowned Anglo-African composer Samuel Coleridge-Taylor came to the United States to conduct his work *The Childhood of Hiawatha* in 1904, Clough was one of the featured soloists. The concert was given in Washington, D.C. J. Arthur Freeman and Harry T. Burleigh were the other soloists. Clough continued her concert singing career during the years that followed. In the 1930s she formed her own voice studio in Worcester.

SOURCES

Southern, Eileen, *Biographical Dictionary of Afro-American and African Musicians* (Westport, CT: Greenwood Press, 1982), 74.

Inez Clough
(c. 1860s/'70s—1933)

Inez Clough was born in New England during the second half of the nineteenth century and died in December of 1933 in Chicago, Illinois. During the 1880s she first attracted attention singing in concerts in Worcester, Massachusetts. During the late 1890s she sang in *Forty Minutes of Grand and Comic Opera* with John Isham's Oriental American Company. She later toured with the company in Europe. When the company returned to the United States at the close of the tour, Clough remained abroad and toured as a music hall entertainer for a five-year period. Upon her return to the United States she joined the company of George Walker and Bert Williams, appearing in *In Dahomey* (1902–1904), *In Abyssinia* (1906–1907), and *In Bandanna Land* (1907–1909). In 1906 she appeared in the musical *Shoo Fly Regiment* by Bob Cole, Rosamund Johnson, and James Weldon Johnson. Clough also appeared as a concert soloist in New York, Washington, D.C, and other major cities in the east. She became a charter member of the Original Lafayette Players in 1913, and in the 1920s sang on Broadway in works such as *Shuffle Along* (1921) by Noble Sissle and Eubie Blake, and their 1924 production *The Chocolate Dandies.*

SOURCES

Southern, Eileen, *Biographical Dictionary of Afro-American and African Musicians* (Westport, CT: Greenwood Press, 1982), 74–75.

Cleota J. Collins
(1893–1976)

Soprano Cleota Collins was born on September 24, 1893, in Cleveland, Ohio. As the story goes, her father, Reverend Ira A. Collins, discovered her vocal talent. Reverend Collins heard someone singing in the yard outside of the church. When he ventured to find the source of the singing he saw his daughter bowing to an imaginary, but most gracious audience. She went on to study at Ohio State University. Cleota Collins had the good fortune of becoming the protégée of Madame E. Azalia

Hackley. This relationship enabled Collins to study abroad in France and Italy. Mrs. Harvey Goulder and Mrs. S.E. Ferris, wealthy music lovers, were also patrons of Cleota Collins. She went on to teach at Florida Baptist College; Sam Houston College in Austin, Texas; and Virginia State College, where she was head of the voice department. She was also one of the founders of the National Association of Negro Musicians. She died on July 7, 1976, in Pasadena, California.

SOURCES

Lovinggood, P., *Famous Modern Negro Musicians* (New York, 1921/R1978), 34–37. Obituary: *The Black Perspective in Music,* Vol. 4, No. 3, 344.

Ellabelle Davis
(1907–1960)

Ellabelle Davis I did meet at one time. She was quite a soprano. As a matter of fact, [when I was] a youngster she was singing as guest soloist with the Philadelphia Orchestra, Eugene Ormandy conducting. I went to a matinee and sat up in the top of the Academy of Music there in that balcony. I don't like heights and I was just sitting up there. I felt like a bird. And this woman came out, sang *Ritorno vincitor* [from *Aida* by G. Verdi], and just tore it to pieces. You see, all this was before blacks were accepted [in the United States] to do opera.

— William Warfield, April 21, 1994

Ellabelle Davis, soprano, was born in New Rochelle, New York, on March 17, 1907. Her father was a local grocer, and Davis worked as a seamstress in order to pay for her early voice lessons. She would become one of the most prominent African American singers in the United States. In the 1920s she studied with Reina LeZar and performed with her sister Marie, a pianist. In New York she studied with William Patterson. On October 25, 1942, Davis made her historic Town Hall debut in New York. By the time of her third Town Hall recital, two years later, she'd become so popular that seats were placed on the stage in order to accommodate the audience overflow. On June 23, 1946, she made her operatic debut as *Aida* at the Opera Nacional in Mexico City. That same year she appeared at the Teatro Gran Rex in Buenos Aires. The League of Composers voted

Portrait of Ellabelle Davis, soprano. Courtesy of the E. Azalia Hackley Collection, Detroit Public Library.

Davis the American singer of the year for the 1946–1947 season and commissioned a composition in her honor. Lukas Foss, as a result, composed *The Song of Songs,* a solo cantata for soprano and orchestra. Davis performed the work in 1947 with Serge Koussevitsky and the Boston Symphony. From 1946 on she toured with pianist Kelley Wyatt throughout the United States, Europe, South America, Central America, Mexico, and

Israel. In 1948 she debuted at historic Carnegie Hall in New York. The following year she debuted at the equally historic La Scala in Milan, Italy, singing *Aida* once again. In 1950 she was soloist at the Berkshire Music Festival, and in 1959 performed with the National Symphony Orchestra singing Richard Strauss's *Four Last Songs.* Ellabelle Davis died of cancer at the New Rochelle Hospital on November 15, 1960. She was 53 years old.

SOURCES

De Lerma, Dominique-René, *The New Grove Dictionary of American Music* (New York: St. Martin's Press, 1986), Vol. 1, 584.
Obituary: *Musical America,* December 1960, 96.
Southern, Eileen, *Biographical Dictionary of Afro-American and African Musicians* (Westport, CT: Greenwood Press, 1982), 94–95.

"Davis at Stadium August 1; 32nd Season Opens June 20," *New York Amsterdam News,* 4 June 1949, 4

Fresh from new triumphs in Europe, Ellabelle Davis, distinguished American soprano, will be added to the 1949 roster of Stadium Concerts with her appearance at Lewisohn Stadium scheduled for Monday night August 1, with Efrem Kurts directing the New York Philharmonic-Symphony Orchestra.

Already a number of local organizations are planning the purchase of blocks of tickets for the inclusion of the Davis debut August 1, as a tribute to the success of a great artist of the race and as a means of adding a substantial sum to charity funds.

"Ellabelle Davis to Sing Lewisohn Stadium Aug. 1," *New York Amsterdam News,* 30 July 1949, 13

Ellabelle Davis, internationally famous star of concert and opera, will make her debut at Lewisohn Stadium Concerts, Monday evening, August 1, with the New York Philharmonic-Symphonic Orchestra under the baton of Efrem Kurtz.

Miss Davis will be heard in New York City for the first time since her extensive and successful concert tour of Europe where she sang more than sixty recitals and orchestral concerts throughout the continent and the British Isles, distinguished by her appearances at the Schevinengin Festival in Holland and at the Prague Festival where she drew the largest attendance record of the festival.

In Paris she received the adoration of the music-loving French people, and after singing with leading symphony orchestras and in concert halls, was immediately engaged for return dates at the Salle Gaveau. Edward

Pendleton reported in the Paris edition of the *New York Herald Tribune*, "From the very first notes, Miss Davis cast a spell over the audience. She has a voice of gold." In the British Isles, her tour was marked by appearances with the BBC Symphony and concerts in leading music centers.

Following her Stadium concert, Miss Davis is scheduled for an orchestral concert at Hollywood Bowl, Los Angeles, under the direction of Iszler Solomorf, conductor of the Columbus Symphony Orchestra, which is sponsored by the National Association of Negro Musicians, convening in that city August 21–26.

The first half of the Stadium concert will list orchestral works conducted by Mr. Kurtz; Bizet's Symphony in C major and the first Stadium performance of Villa-Lobos' "Uirapura." After the intermission, Miss Davis will sing two operatic arias, "Ritorna Vincitor" from Verdi's "Aida" and "Casta Diva" from Bellini's "Norma." Following the Overture, "I Vespri Siciliani" by Verdi, Miss Davis will close the program with two Negro spirituals, "Nobody Knows the Trouble I Seen," arranged, by Burleigh, and Hall Johnson's "Honor! Honor!"

"Ellabelle Davis, Soprano, Kaufmann Auditorium, March 8," *Musical America,* March 1954, 30

Ellabelle Davis' program, consisting entirely of lieder, featured Schumann's cycle *Frauenliebe und Leben* and was rounded out with groups by Schubert, Hugo Wolf, and Richard Strauss.

The soprano's performances were uniformly remarkable for sensitive phrasing, unfailing taste, and emotional conviction. Even in the opening Schubert group, where the singer had yet to achieve complete breath control and warmth of vocal quality, the stylistic security of her approach and the meaningful molding of every detail made for beguiling interpretations. In the ensuing Schumann cycle the voice emerged freely and fully and the results were nothing short of inspired. The inner radiance of Miss Davis' interpretation of the Schumann cycle seemed to carry past the intermission into the long group of Wolf lieder that opened the second half of the recital. She managed to convey in each of eight songs of widely contrasting moods not only the right atmosphere but also a sense that each of the songs was of supreme importance. Arpad Sandor was the sympathetic accompanist.

— A.B.

Harry Delmore

Harry Delmore, dramatic tenor, studied with Arthur Wilson of Boston and other teachers of standing. After touring extensively throughout the northern and southern United States, Delmore gave his debut recital at Jordan Hall in Boston on October 18, 1925. In January of 1932 he went to Milan, Italy, for additional training in the field of opera. Upon his return he taught privately in the Boston area. Among performances following his return to the United States were a return engagement at Jordan Hall and appearances with the People's Symphony Orchestra.

SOURCES

Cuney-Hare, Maud: *Negro Musicians and Their Music* (Washington, D.C.: Da Capo Press, 1936).

Lurena Wallace Dethridge

Natives of Richmond, Indiana, soprano Dethridge's parents were early settlers who followed Quaker traditions and teachings. She received her formal education in Chattanooga, Tennessee. S.B. Garton, a respected voice teacher in the Richmond, area advised Dethridge to study voice after hearing her sing and being moved by her vocal talents. She subsequently studied voice with Garton and later in Italy. She appeared in recitals in Rome, where she also studied for eight months, and in the United States. Dethridge later returned to Rome for additional vocal and linguistic study and gave a recital in the Sala Sgambati.

SOURCES

Cuney-Hare, Maud, *Negro Musicians and Their Music* (Washington, D.C.: Da Capo Press, 1936), 379–380.

Todd Duncan
(1903 — 1998)

I got to know Todd Duncan actually through William Duncan Allen, who was his accompanist all the time. And they went to Australia because I remember they went to Australia and New Zealand together. Todd made quite a tour of Australia and New Zealand. And then after my debut in 1950 I was hired by the Australian Broadcasting Commission and went on sort of the same tour [through] some of the same cities that Todd and Bill Allen had been on, except I didn't go to New Zealand. And I met friends that took me over into their arms that were friends of Todd Duncan.

Todd was at my Town Hall debut in 1950. He embraced me as an older artist. When he was doing *Lost in the Stars* I was there and saw him and went back to his dressing room. To this day I call Todd and talk.

When they did *Porgy and Bess,* with Todd, direction and production wise, staging wise the star always had some kind of a spot [light] or something. That was just a foregone conclusion. And Todd came to see my production at the National Theatre in Washington [D.C.] in 1952. And Todd came back and said, "Man, you better tell them folks to put some light on you. They got you in the dark half the time." And I said, "Well, it's supposed to be that way, Todd. I'm not important when I'm in the dark." He said, "Porgy ought to always be lit." He's from the old school and he was very outspoken like that. Have you read anything about his interviews with Gershwin? Somebody said, "This Gershwin wants you."

TODD DUNCAN: "Who is he?"

SOMEBODY: "He writes [such and such]."

TODD DUNCAN: "Oh, you mean that honky-tonk! I ain't got nothin' to do with him."

He took that attitude, you know. He went down there with that *I Am Mr. Duncan* you know and then walked away just totally in love with George Gershwin as he was playing the score for him. That was typical of Todd. I think Todd would've been the typical kind of person that would've gone to church and if you'd done any Gospel [music] back in his church he would've said *Put him out!* He was this kind of a person. Very elegant, top standard, and of course a fabulous artist. Todd and I have been friends all these years.

Todd Duncan was there with Anne Brown at the Metropolitan [as special guests in attendance for the Met premier of *Porgy and Bess*]. They had them sitting right on the first row. Todd was with Gladys, his wife. Then another friend of mine actually was the escort for Anne Brown. Todd has a voice like me, you know. I try to whisper and if I whisper everybody hears around and just cracks up, if I'm saying something I'm not supposed to be saying. So, Todd was there and Porgy comes home, you know, at the end and says, "Just you wait till that gal sees me." And he takes out this red dress that he had bought. And without trying to whisper — you know Grace [Bumbry, who portrayed Bess at the Met premier] is not exactly what you'd call a small woman, Todd said to Gladys, "Hm, hm! That woman'll never fit into that dress." And the whole front row collapsed.

— *William Warfield, April 21, 1994*

Robert Todd Duncan, baritone, was born in Danville, Kentucky, on February 12, 1903. In 1925 he received a Bachelor of Arts degree from Butler University in Indiana. In 1930 he graduated from Columbia University Teachers College with a master's degree. His vocal instructors were Sara Lee, Edward Lippe, and Sidney Dietch. On July 10, 1934, Duncan made his debut in opera as Alfio in Mascagni's *Cavalleria Rusticana* with the Aeolian Opera in New York. The following year he created one of the most famous roles in the history of American opera, Porgy in George Gershwin's *Porgy and Bess.* The first performance took place at New York's Alvin Theatre on October 10, 1935. He repeated the role in 1937 and 1942. Todd Duncan was also active in musical theater and film. In 1938 he appeared in the London production of *The Sun Never Sets,* in 1940 he appeared as the Lord's General in *Cabin in the Sky,* by Vernon Duke, at the Martin Beck Theatre, and as Stephen Kumalo in *Lost in the Stars* at New York's Music Box. The show ran from October 30, 1949, to April 3, 1950, and earned Duncan the Donaldson and New York Drama Critics awards in 1950.

Robert Todd Duncan became the first African American male to sing with a major

Portrait of Todd Duncan. Photographs and Prints Division, Schomburg Center for Research in Black Culture, The New York Public Library, Astor, Lenox and Tilden Foundations.

opera company, when he sang the role of Tonio in Leoncavallo's *I Pagli-acci* with the New York City Opera Company in 1945. He also sang the role of Escamillo in Bizet's *Carmen* during the 1945 season. His New York Town Hall debut took place in 1944. His film credits include *Syncopation* in 1942 and *Unchained* in 1955. Duncan and his accompanist and close friend, William Duncan Allen, gave numerous recitals throughout the United States and abroad. At the time of his retirement, as a performer, Duncan had given more than 2,000 recitals in 56 countries. Todd Duncan taught at Louisville Municipal College for Negroes from 1925 to 1930, at Howard University in Washington, D.C. from 1931 to 1945, and at the Curtis Institute in Philadelphia. He received an honorary doctorate from Howard University in 1938, was honored by the Washington Performing Arts Society in 1978, and received the George Peabody Medal in 1984.

SOURCES

Cuney-Hare, Maud, *Negro Musicians and Their Music* (Washington, D.C.: Da Capo Press, 1936), 380.
De Lerma, Dominique-René, *The New Grove Dictionary of American Music* (New York: St. Martin's Press, 1986), Vol. 1, 660–661.
Southern, Eileen, *Biographical Dictionary of Afro-American and African Musicians* (Westport, CT: Greenwood Press, 1982), 118.

New York Amsterdam News, 15 July 1939, 17

It's been a long time since Todd Duncan the "Porgy and Bess" star has made a local appearance. He is scheduled to appear as one of the guest soloists Monday night at the second anniversary memorial for George Gershwin at the Lewisohn Stadium, 137th Street and Amsterdam Avenue. Anne Brown who sang opposite Mr. Duncan in the original Gershwin opera and the famous Eva Jessye Choir are also on the program.

"Todd Duncan in Superb Concert," *New York Amsterdam News,* 6 January 1940, 20

Todd Duncan, baritone artist/teacher, treated a capacity audience of 500 to ninety minutes of superb music on New Year's night at the Harlem Y.M.C.A., where he was presenting under the joint auspices of the "Y" and the Citizens' Cooperating Committee.

A specialist in character numbers, Mr. Duncan gave a program that easily merits a Carnegie Hall appearance. Moussorgsky's "Song of the Flea," with its trick musical laughter; Tierot's "Briolage," in which a French farmer calls affectionately to his oxen to plow the fields, and Saint-Saens' "Danse Macabre," built on the theme that Death tunes his violin and skeletons dance among tombstones, were highlights of the official program. Each was a gem unto itself, artistic courage being required for their interpretation.

"Todd Duncan Plans European Tour,"
Musical America, 25 April 1947, 17

Todd Duncan, baritone, will be the only American-born and trained artist to appear in recital at the Edinburgh International Festival of Music, to be held in Scotland in August and September. In recitals in England and the continent, which he will give on his forthcoming tour, Mr. Duncan plans to include the music of his race, including spirituals, some of the unusual and beautiful Creole songs of Louisiana, and folksongs of Haiti in the patios of that island. These will be in addition to the classical works, the later Romantic art songs and Lieder from his repertoire.

Mr. Duncan will also appear in opera in cities abroad, singing the role of Amonasro in Aida, and other parts. In many of the opera houses it will be the first time that a Negro has sung the part of the Ethiopian king, a role for which the light-skinned baritone finds it necessary to use dark make-up.

The singer will appear in both Amsterdam and The Hague in Holland, probably prior to the Edinburgh Festival, and will then go to Scandinavia, singing in both opera and concert in Stockholm and Copenhagen, Denmark, on Oct. 8. In the early part of October he will return to the Low Countries, singing in Brussels, Antwerp, Ostend and Knocke, Belgium.

He will be heard as soloist with the BBC Symphony in a broadcast on Oct. 27 and will make his formal debut in England on Nov. 2 at the Royal Albert Hall in concert. For the next three weeks he will tour the country, appearing in most of the large cities, including Newcastle, Sheffield, Birmingham, Leicester, Liverpool, and Glasgow, Scotland.

At the end of November Mr. Duncan will appear in two concerts in each of the cities of Vienna and Budapest; then in December he will go to Italy, singing in Rome, Florence, Turin and probably Milan, in both concerts and opera.

Before he departs for his strenuous tour, the baritone will make several appearances with summer symphony orchestras throughout the United States, and he will coach with Laszlo Halasz, artistic director and conductor of the New York City Opera Company, for his appearances in opera abroad.

"Todd Duncan, Baritone, Town Hall, Nov. 18,"
Musical America, 15 December 1951, 12

Although he has sung extensively in New York in recent years, this was only Todd Duncan's second recital here and his first since 1944. In the interim he has concertized extensively both in this country and in Latin America, sung on numerous radio programs, and appeared on Broadway in Kurt Weill's *Lost in the Stars*. A large and extremely cordial audience was on hand to greet him.

The program he presented was serious and tastefully ordered and the dignity of his presence coupled with the concentration and musicality with which he approached everything in it made for rewarding inter-pretations. His voice was still warming up in Bach's "So wundre Dich, O Meister nicht," J. W. Franck's "Oh Let Us Praise the Lord," and "Secchi's Love Me or Not," but the clarity of diction and the intelligence of his musicianship were gratifyingly apparent.

Seven songs from Schubert's *Die Schone Mullerin* followed. Here too Mr. Duncan's performances were marked by clear and understanding projection of the texts and all comprehension of line. In the vigorous declamation that he brought to such songs as "Das Wandern" and "Am Feierabend" his tones were clear and ringing, but the soft, spun-out mezza voce of other songs, notably "Halt!" and "Der Neugierige," they became breathy and monotonous in color and tended to sag below pitch. The same difficulty was apparent in two of the three Wolf lieder that came just before intermission, but Der Rattenfanger rang out superbly.

The second half was given over entirely to songs in English — perhaps the finest performance of them all was of Rachmaninoff's "O Thou Bil-lowly Harvest Field." Moussorgsky's "The Seminarist" and two Delius songs, all very well sung indeed, led to two folk songs, the prayer from *Lost in the Stars*, and two spirituals. There were several encores. William Allen provided extremely musical, if not always technically impeccable, accompaniments.

"Baritone Saga," *Musical America*, 1 February 1955, 10 and 13

Twice the old community of Danville, Ky, since its settlement in 1775, has been touched by history. Once because its tiny Centre College defeated Harvard in a football game — but then, almost every other team in the country has done likewise at one time or another. And once because (Robert) Todd Duncan was born here — although he left the Blue Grass country 19 months later and didn't return to it for a dozen years, and then not for long.

Qualifications aside, Danville claims Todd as a native son. And well he may, for his roots are there, and he is the rare kind of man and artist to whom strange and healthy roots are important. There is no significant growth without them, and Todd Duncan has grown, artistically and oth-erwise, every year of his distinguished life.

Lincoln's birthday was Todd's own — in 1903. The coincidence argued well for the boy. The principles that motivated the Emancipator are his, too, not by osmosis, but by dint of a gifted and tenacious mind that did not demean itself to accept less than its due, or to compromise a particle of hard-earned integrity.

Todd's father was a garageman, neither poor nor well to do. He lives now in retirement at Indianapolis, whither he brought Todd as an infant. Perhaps symbolically, it was the boy's happy lot to begin his education in a nonsegregated school system, which has since gone into segregation and back out of it again. His grade school was P.S. 23. Just before he was graduated, Indiana went "separate but equal," and Todd remembers without malice that the move was precipitated by pressure in behalf of unemployed Negro teachers. By the time he was ready for junior high, it was a colored school, at West and 10th, to which he was assigned. After that he was sent to Louisville, 70 miles north of his hometown, to attend a prep school euphemistically known as Simmons College. After graduation he went to Butler University, in Indiana, where he won his A.B. as an English major in 1925.

Classroom to "Cavalleria." For more than a dozen years afterward, Todd Duncan's identity was mostly pedagogical, with multiple brief interruptions. First he went back to Simmons, where for five academic years he taught English and music (he had studied the latter informally with his music teaching mother). In 1930 he came to Columbia University for an M.A., again in English. In 1931 he joined the music faculty of Howard University, in Washington, D.C., which was soon to realize what a volatile talent it had taken under its wing.

In June of 1934, when he had married Gladys Jackson Tignor, of Charlottesville, Va., herself a teacher, Todd requested and got a leave to try out for the role of Alfio in a special all-Negro "Cavalleria Rusticana" that was being prepared for the Mecca Temple, now the New York City Center. His friend Abbie Mitchell, who got him the audition, soon was to play a far more significant part in the shaping of Todd's professional career.

"Cavalleria" came off as scheduled without event, and he returned to Howard for the winter semester. Unbeknownst to him, George Gershwin was then looking desperately for a singer to create the male lead in "Porgy and Bess." Abbie Mitchell suggested to the composer that Duncan, who had acquitted himself so well as her Alfio, might be the man he needed. The composer, pressed for time and getting nowhere with his search after a full year of auditioning, agreed to hear him.

In the late summer of 1935, on a Sunday afternoon, Todd presented himself at the entrance to Gershwin's penthouse in the East 70s. In short order he found that he had made two mistakes. First, he had not brought any accompanist with him. (His answer to this was approximately: "But you play, don't you?" Gershwin did.) Second, he had chosen only the most severely classical material, which he proceeded to sing in the appropriate manner. Gershwin was too dumbfounded to do anything but comply gracefully with Todd's suggestion that they begin at once. And then, before the composer could register any annoyance, the young baritone was spinning out the most beautiful of arie antiche, specifically Secchi's "Lungi dal caro bene," just as beautifully as it deserved. Gershwin was impressed by the quality of Todd's voice, despite the stiffness of his platform poise. When it was over, the composer inquired whether or not he had prepared any spirituals. The answer was a firm, disapproving negative.

Ignoring the reproof, Gershwin asked him to come back the following Sunday for a final audition with the show's backers. Todd refused flatly; he had a church solo to do at home. The composer pressed the point; how about the Sunday after that? That could be arranged. Todd said, "But Mr. Gershwin, I am just a teacher and I can't afford to be making trips like this for the fun of it." Would $35 cover the expenses? Comfortably. A check was promptly made out in that amount, and the date was set.

At the time, the magic of Gershwin's name meant very little to Professor Duncan, improbable as that might seem at this distance. His life was far removed from Broadway and all that it connoted. He had heard of Gershwin, but he hadn't liked what music of his had come to his attention. He wasn't at all sure that "Porgy" was enough to warrant his departing the security of the Howard campus, or that he should accept an offer to sing any such "trash"—his own contemporary description—for any amount of money.

Still, at the appointed hour, Todd was back at Gershwin's penthouse. Little did he appreciate the flattery of having such a battery of eminences on hand to witness his test run. Many glittering names in the old high echelon of the Theatre Guild were present—some of the most important people in show business. Innocent of these somewhat frightening circumstances, Todd again sailed into his arie antiche, and then Gershwin started going through the "Porgy" score for the visitor's benefit.

Just before the composer plunged into "I Got Plenty o' Nuttin," he paused for a moment, looked deep into Todd's skeptical eyes, and remarked that this song would make the singer a famous man. Then he bolted into the plink-plank introductory measures, whereupon the singer—to his mortification ever after—was heard to exclaim questioningly, as if by reflex action: "That?"

At least, the music sounded to Todd eminently singable, if not exactly what he had in mind; and he quickly decided that he could not afford to turn down the generous offer made to him that afternoon. The short of it is that "Porgy" opened in Boston that September, moved to New York a month later, and had only a short run. Like so many lyric masterworks, it was ahead of its time. But Gershwin had been right about "I Got Plenty o' Nuttin'." On opening night, and every night thereafter, this number stopped the show, and it proved to be the cornerstone of Todd Duncan's subsequent fame.

The spring of 1936 found him back at Howard. A year later he was off again, this time for a gala concert with the Los Angeles Philharmonic, with Gershwin conducting. It was a huge success, and the $35,000 party that followed it that night at the Trocadero was one of the most stupendous in the history of a city that is known for its super-functions. It was, unfortunately, to be Gershwin's last. He died a few months later, unaware that "Porgy" would become a modern classic.

Todd, for his part, was ready to resume his professorial duties after a short vacation. But some time was to intervene before he got back to Howard. This time it was an offer from Merle Armitage, then planning a West Coast revival of "Porgy" that stayed his pedagogical urge. An "act of God," as the law puts it, threw a monkey wrench into the project; the production suffered from the worst weather California had ever seen. Every backer lost his investment, and Todd began to think seriously of abandoning all thoughts of a stage career. Then, just as he was about to head east, the publisher Max Dreyfus called from New York to relay an offer from his producer/brother in London. Would he be interested in a part in "The Sun Never Sets," scheduled for that autumn in Drury Lane? He would!

A year afterward (late in 1938), Todd left England and came back to Howard; and this time he had every intention of staying put. Perhaps his resolve was influenced by a certain amount of conscience for having so tried the patience of his long-suffering dean.

Destiny apparently never meant Duncan to spend his life as a teacher, and two years after this last noble attempt, he said his last goodbye to the campus that had been his home during most of his musical life. The role that lured him away was the Lawd's General in "Cabin in the Sky" —one of his most notable characterizations. The next season, 1942, Cheryl Crawford cast him as Porgy in her now legendary revival. With that the wheel of fortune came to rest irrevocably on baritone Todd Duncan, erstwhile professor.

In 1944, he gave Miss Crawford what must have been the most generous notice of resignation in the annals of the theatre: In six months, he said, he was going to quit, and would she please start looking for another Porgy?

At this writing, Mr. Duncan has rounded out an even decade as a concert artist, with occasional time out for special operatic appearances and for such a notable portrayal as he gave in "Lost in the Stars," the musical play by Maxwell Anderson and the late Kurt Weill based on Alan Paton's novel "Cry, the Beloved Country." He has toured as far afield as Australia and New Zealand, reaped more honor than many a name singer has in a full-length career, and known more happiness than comes to most of us in an entire lifetime.

There is no space here to deal adequately with Todd Duncan the man. This is too bad, because he is a singularly human person, with a heart and an intellect as big as his frame, and the voice that gives it meaning. Someday I mean to drop by at his big brick house on T Street in Washington, D.C., or at his summer place in Arundel, near Annapolis, to see his home life at closest range. And someday I would like to meet his boy; Charles Todd graduated from Dartmouth and Harvard Law School, who now works for the National Association for the Advancement of Colored People. If he is a chip off the old block, we need not fear for the advancement of any people who can boast such eloquent representation in the human race.

For Todd Duncan is, more than a fine artist, a gentleman and a scholar, and it is a pleasure to be in his company.

Simon Estes
(1938–)

Bass-baritone Simon Lamont Estes was born on February 2, 1938, in Centerville, Iowa. While a student at the University of Iowa he studied with Charles Kellis. A scholarship enabled him to continue his studies at the Juilliard School in New York in 1964. After studying abroad he made his professional debut as Ramfis in Aida with the Deutsche Opera in Berlin in 1965. He also sang at Lubeck and at Hamburg. In 1966 Estes won a medal at the first Tchaikovsky Vocal Competition in Moscow. This led to appearances throughout Europe and North America. Estes became the first African American male to take a major role at Bayreuth, in 1978. He sang the title role in Wagner's *Der fliegende Hollander*. He considers this to be his best and most demanding role. In 1982 Estes debuted at the Metropolitan Opera in New York as the Landgrave in *Tannhäuser*. Other roles include Philip II, Wotan, Oroveso, Boris, Porgy and the four villains in *Les contes d'Hoffmann*. He sang the role of Amonasro to Leontyne Price's Aida for her final operatic appearance in 1985 at the Met. Since that time he joined the vocal faculty at Juilliard. Estes has throughout his career been an outspoken defender of African American male singers and has often criticized the opera companies throughout the United States for what he sees as their lackluster effort in addressing the problem.

SOURCES

Hitchcock, H. Wiley, and Stanley Sadie, eds., *The New Grove Dictionary of American Music,* (London: Macmillan, 1986).
Smith, Eric Ledell, *Blacks in Opera: An Encyclopedia of People and Companies, 1873–1993* (Jefferson, N.C.: McFarland, 1994).

Lillian Evanti
(1890–1967)

I met Evanti and was even in a performance with her once in Washington, D.C. She was a gorgeous person, just absolutely, and sang like an angel. She was very fair, you know, and I've heard people say that when she went to Italy that's why, I think, she changed her name to Evanti instead of Evans, Lillian Evans. Did you know that? Her name was supposedly Lillian Evans, and she went to Rome and came back as Madame Evanti. And the European friends of mine that knew her said the Europeans were very confused. They didn't know what she was. Was she white? Was she black? You know! She was one of those people who was very fair, straight hair with curls and all that sort of thing. And what with the barrier being an opera star, and nobody black being in opera, they were totally in the dark in Europe as to what she was, but Madame Evanti was something.

— *William Warfield, April 21, 1994*

Lillian Evanti (also known as Lillian Evans) was born on August 12, 1890, in Washington, D.C. The coloratura soprano received a Bachelor of Music degree in 1917 from the Howard University School of Music in Washington, D.C. While at that institution she studied with Lulu Vere Childers. In November of 1915 she performed with violinist Felix Weir and attracted the attention of the public for the first time.

Eventually Evanti went to Europe for further vocal study. From 1925 to 1930 she studied with Madame Ritter-Ciampi in Paris and with Rosa

Storchio in Italy. In 1925 she sang the title role in Delibes' opera *Lakme* in Nice, France, at the Casino Theatre, and repeated the role in 1927 in Paris at the Trianon Lyrique. Numerous performances throughout her career took Evanti to the Caribbean, South America, parts of Europe and the United States as well. In February of 1934 the soprano sang for Eleanor Roosevelt and her guests at the White House. In 1943 she sang the role of Violetta in Verdi's *La Traviata* with the renowned Mary Cardwell Dawson National Negro Opera Company in Washington, D.C., Frederick Vajda directed the production. Evanti was once married to the noted organist and teacher Roy Wilford Tibbs. She died on December 7, 1967, in Washington, D.C.

SOURCES

Cuney-Hare, Maud, *Negro Musicians and Their Music* (Washington, D.C.: Da Capo Press, 1936), 357–358.
Southern, Eileen, *Biographical Dictionary of Afro-American and African Musicians* (Westport, CT: Greenwood Press, 1982), 129–130.

"Crisis Keeps Evanti In West Indies Isle," *New York Amsterdam News,* 16 September 1939, 5

Port of Spain (By Cable to *The Amsterdam News*)— Among the large number of American citizens still unable to get passage to the United States because of the European war is Lillian Evanti, international lyric coloratura soprano. She is on the Island of Trinidad, West Indies.

Mme. Evanti came in last week from Venezuela aboard the S.S. Uraquay, the Columbia received orders to "stay where you are" and for three days the ship was marooned in the Caribbean with an international passenger list.

Putting in a bid immediately for a cabin on several liners due to sail for New York, Evanti discovered that all of them are booked solid with passengers trying to get back to the United States. Accommodations on the S.S. Brazil are definitely uncertain; the S.S. Argentina is filled to capacity, it was learned.

However, the Washington singer hopes to get passage on the S.S. Iroquois, which cruises to Puerto Rico, Martinique, St. Thomas and Bermuda. It is due in New York on Saturday, September 16.

While on a South American concert tour, the soprano was heralded in many cities. Her appearance in Trinidad was at the Royal Theatre.

Mme. Evanti has sung throughout Europe, being a favorite in England and Italy. In 1934, at the invitation of Mrs. Franklin D. Roosevelt, she sang at the White House. On one of her trips to Europe she was accompanied by Thurlow, who is now a Harvard University student. The estranged wife of Roy Tibbs, head of the music department of Howard "U," Mme. Evanti and her mother, Mrs. Bruce Evans, live at 1910 Vermont Avenue, in Washington, D.C.

William Franklin
(1906–)

He was born in Memphis, Tennessee, and raised in Chicago, Illinois. The Chicago area served as the arena for his early musical training. While attending Wendell Phillips High School, he was coached by Mildred Bryant Jones and played in various instrumental ensembles.

Upon completion of his high school education he embarked on a jazz career playing trombone and singing with various groups. From 1925 to 1935 Franklin worked with jazz leaders of the age, such as Clarence Jones, Dave Peyton, Stanley "Fess" Williams and Earl "Fatha" Hines. An injury sustained from an automobile accident brought his trombone playing to an end. He then decided to continue his vocal training.

At the Chicago Conservatory of Music he studied with Alexander Carado and others as well. With the Chicago Civic Opera he made his operatic debut in 1937 singing Amonasro in Verdi's *Aida*. La Julia Rhea sang the title role. The success of this venture enabled Franklin to tour widely as a concert singer. He sang in numerous operas and musicals. Many of his stage performances were with Mary Caldwell Dawson's National Negro Opera Company. One of his most popular stage interpretations was the title role in Gilbert and Sullivan's *The Mikado*.

SOURCES
Southern, Eileen, *Biographical Dictionary of Afro-American and African Musicians* (Westport, CT: Greenwood Press, 1982), 137–138.

George Garner

George Garner, tenor, who graduated in 1918 from the Chicago Musical College, was one of the leading African American singers of his day.

He received a Bachelor of Music degree from the American Conservatory of Music in June of 1926. Pauline Bell Garner, his wife and a talented pianist in her own right, often appeared with George Garner as his accompanist. She graduated from Northwestern University. Five thousand dollars were raised privately for Garner, enabling him to study abroad with one of England's most respected musicians, Sir Roger Quilter. Later he appeared as tenor soloist with the Chicago Symphony Orchestra, the result of a competition. Throughout 1932 many concert engagements took place.

SOURCES

Cuney-Hare, Maud, *Negro Musicians and Their Music* (Washington, D.C.: Da Capo Press, 1936), 379.

John Greene
(1901—1960s)

Baritone John Greene was born in 1901 in Columbus, Ohio, and died in Los Angeles, California, in the 1960s. Settling in Chicago, Illinois, in the 1920s, Greene studied at the Cosmopolitan School of Music. Numbered among his teachers were George Garner and T. Theodore Taylor. In 1931 he won first place in a Kraft Music Hall competition and sang on various Kraft radio broadcasts on station WMAQ. In 1933 Greene received a Julius Rosenwald, fellowship enabling him to finish his studies. An additional fellowship followed in 1934. As time went by, Greene developed a reputation throughout the Chicago area as a first-class singer. He toured extensively as bass-baritone for the National Cash Register Company. He settled in Los Angeles, California, in the 1950s.

SOURCES

Cuney-Hare, Maud, *Negro Musicians and Their Music* (Washington, D.C.: Da Capo Press, 1936), 382.
Southern, Eileen, *Biographical Dictionary of Afro-American and African Musicians* (Westport, CT: Greenwood Press, 1982), 153.

Elizabeth Taylor Greenfield
(c1819–1876)

Elizabeth Taylor Greenfield was born a slave in Natchez, Mississippi. While still a child she was freed and taken to Philadelphia by her mistress, Elizabeth H. Greenfield. Her mistress, a Quaker, sponsored her education. The young girl learned to play the guitar, harp, and piano. Also, she studied voice briefly with a local amateur. She made attempts to further her education while in Philadelphia, but was unsuccessful in doing so. After the death of her patron in 1844, she settled in Buffalo, New York. The Buffalo Musical Association encouraged her to further her development and sponsored her debut concert in October of 1851. This concert and numerous Taylor-Greenfield concerts, which followed, were reported in Frederick Douglass's *North Star*. The *Buffalo Commercial Advertiser* dubbed her "The Black Swan." For the next two years she was managed by Colonel J.H. Wood and toured extensively. With the help of patrons, Taylor-Greenfield went to Europe, arriving in London on April 16, 1853. With the aid of Harriet Beecher Stowe and the Duchess of Sutherland, the soprano was able to perform and survive financially during her stay. On May 10, 1854, Taylor-Greenfield gave a command performance for her Majesty, Queen Victoria, at Buckingham Palace. Sir George Smart, organist and composer to her Majesty's Chapel Royal, accompanied her. Upon her return to the United States, in the summer of 1854, she continued a concert career that lasted an additional two decades. Her tours took her to such places as Michigan in 1855, Wisconsin in 1857, and Montreal in 1863. She eventually settled in Philadelphia, where she opened a voice studio. Among her pupils were Carrie Thomas and Thomas J. Bowers. Elizabeth Taylor-Greenfield was the first African American concert singer to achieve success in her field in Europe and the United States. She died on March 31, 1876, in Philadelphia, Pennsylvania.

SOURCES

Austin, William W., *The New Grove Dictionary of American Music* (New York: St. Martin's Press, 1986), Vol. 2, 285.
Cuney-Hare, Maud, *Negro Musicians and Their Music* (Washington, D.C.: Da Capo Press, 1936), 202–204.
Southern, Eileen, *Biographical Dictionary of Afro-American and African Musicians* (Westport, CT: Greenwood Press, 1982), 153–154.

"Miss Greenfield's Concert." 6, 30 September 1854, p. 250.

"We unfortunately arrived too late Wednesday evening for the more

Portrait of Elizabeth Taylor Greenfield. Photographs and Prints Division, Schomburg Center for Research in Black Culture, The New York Public Library, Astor, Lenox and Tilden Foundations.

important items of the programme, such as 'I know that my Redeemer,' 'Robert,' &c. Yet we heard enough to show the voice and execution of the singer. Her compass is wonderful. In a song called 'I am free,' she commenced in a deep man's voice, which is of course exceptional and far from agreeable in the lowest tones. But suddenly she pitched up to a high soprano, which seemed to proceed from another person, and alternated duet-like as between a male and female voice. Some of the middle and high tones surprised us by their beauty and sweetness, as well as by their remarkable power. They were delivered with a really artistic swell and diminuendo, and many highly ornate passages rendered with great beauty; especially those in Bishop's 'Shades of night returning' and a cadenza ending in a very high note, 'Sweet Home,' which she sang with taste and feeling.

Miss Greenfield is a decided African, stout and matronly in form, though young; but her singing is indeed a wonder, in which fastidious ears may find pleasure, and her manner is simple and pleasing. She has profited by her stay in Europe. The Temple was about half filled by an audience composed in about equal proportions of whites and very respectable looking colored people, and we are glad to hear that the concert resulted in some substantial benefit for Mr. Grime's church."

The "Black Swan." The N.Y. Tribune makes the following sensible and humane comment upon this phenomenon.

Metropolitan Hall was well filled on Thursday evening to hear the singing of Elizabeth Greenfield, called otherwise "The Black Swan." The person who does the ornithology for her musical renown should remember that, though a black swan is a *rara avis* (we forbear to give the quotation, believing that certain classical allusions, such as that — Scylla et Charybdis, Ilomo Sum, &c. &c., should enjoy an amnesty,) it does not sing. Its song when dying is the fancy of a poet when lying. But that apart. There is a certain extraordinary interest attached to Miss Elizabeth Greenfield. She belongs to a poor, peeled, defrauded, abused, despised race. A race that in Africa enslaves itself, and has infernal gods that demand human sacrifices. A race that in this country is either manacled or repulsed. To witness this humble creature seeking to be an artist — to enter the arena of a Sontag or Alboni, has its interest. For our part we could not sympathize with the rollicking gaiety of a considerable portion of the audience in seeing her led forward on the platform. Her behavior was strictly in good taste, and gentlemen should not have laughed at her. Had her auditory been the English House of Lords they would have received her with marked respect.

It is hardly necessary to say that we did not expect to find an artist on the occasion. She has a fine voice, but does not know how to use it. Her merit is purity and fullness, not loudness of tone. Her notes are badly formed in the throat, but her intonation is excellent. She sings in a word, like a child. The extent of her voice is great. She takes easily the lowest chalumeau not of the clarionet, and when it is taken it is worth nothing. The idea of a woman's voice is a feminine: anything below that is disgusting: it is as bad as a bride with a beard on her chin and an oath in her mouth. The low not taken in *Brindisi* might have passed simply as a hint; but the infliction of a whole ballad lying in the baritone region between E and E was quite unendurable. We hear a great deal about Woman's sphere. That sphere exists in music, and it is the soprano region of the voice.

What culture may do in the case in hand remains to be seen, but it is certainly a voice that ought to be cultivated in Europe, and ought to stay there. The bills of the Concert stated that no colored persons would be admitted, and a strong police was there in anticipation of riot, which did not happen. Under these circumstances we advise Elizabeth Greenfield to go to Europe and there remain. It may be added that she was encored in singing, and gave satisfaction to her audience, who appeared to recognize her musical position. That she has succeeded to the extent shown is evidence of intellect, which merits development. She has had everything to contend against — an education neglected — a spurned thing in social life; but her ambition has thus far triumphed and we hope to hear a good account of her studies in a country where Alexander Dumas has learned how to read and write.

[Articles on Elizabeth Taylor-Greenfield as they appeared in *J.S. Dwight's Journal of Music* (1852–1881)]

Barrington Guy
(1905–?)

"*High Yaller* Proves as Big a Barrier to Theatre Progress as Ebony Color Skin Barrington Guy, Operatic Possibility Shunned," *New York Amsterdam News*, 22 April 1939, 20

It used to be "I'm barred because I'm black," but in this case the color is high "yaller" and the circumstances, in which the subject of this piece eats his heart out because he is neither white or all–Negro is applicable in many startling ways to Negroes in all walks of life.

How would you like to be raised with members of your race; go to school with them, play with them, and then move into another world where your color blended with the skin of your new associates and everything goes along so beautifully until the ogre of race prejudice rears its ugly head to blow you tumbling down the ladder to the "alley" whence you came?

The story of life across the color line, its climaxes and denouncements has been blazoned across the silver screen as well as inscribed on the printed page. Yet another chapter needs to be written and it concerns itself with Barrington Guy, brilliant baritone, talented legitimate actor and ballet dancer, whose pale skin keeps him in a living hell.

He's too light for a Negro in moving pictures. As a Negro his color is against him on the legitimate stage. The white audiences who support classic singers and operatic performers want singers black or brown in color or definitely Negroid with woolly hair. The crossing of the line completely is not attractive since one would be just another white person looking for a job among millions of others. No wonder Guy, now at the Plantation Club, sits and sucks his thumbs as the years roll on and his ambitions beat their wings in futile fury against the dank, bleak walls of color prejudice.

Guy was well on the way to the top at one time, he tells me, but came back with a sudden plop to the place from whence he started. Born in Washington, January 20, 1905, he is the son of Nathaniel and Louise Antoinette Guy. His dad was an instructor in drama and considered one of the greatest Negro Shakespearian actors of that day. He was the only Negro in those parts to give a Shakespeare drama each year. Young Guy was singing baritone at the age of five and the remarkableness of these phenomena stirred interest among Washingtonians.

He was given an audition at Shubert's Garrick theatre in Washington, and taken for white, he won first prize singing ironically enough "That's Why They Call Me Shine." The following Sunday he was featured as the amateur find of the year.

Was Keith Headliner. Guy says he became a headliner over the old Keith circuit at the age of five. Meanwhile, his parents sent him to the interpretive dancing classes of Cora B. Shreeves. He was giving joint recitals with his father in which he sang and closed in joint recitation of Shakespeare's "Brutus and Cassius" from Julius Ceasar.

Young Guy was doing well in vaudeville until, one day when fifteen years old, the Keith office got a letter that stated that its young headline star was colored. Other letters followed, mostly, Guy said, from the folks in his own neighborhood, some of them pointing out that the senior Guy was a Negro and that his son must have plenty of the blood. It then developed that theatre owners objected to a Negro kissing, dancing with and appearing on the stage with white women and away went Guy.

Studied for Opera. About this time, Guy says he was studying for the Washington Grand Opera Company, under the celebrated voice teacher, Edward Albian and was leading man in Miss Shreeves' juvenile carnival of 200 white kiddies. While on Keith, Guy said he appeared with Ann Sutton, Keith Headliner; Catherine Lyons, winner of the prize as "Miss America" at Atlantic City who was his ex-dancing partner; Vivian Maronelli; Genevieve Pyles, first cousin of Mary Pickford.

"I have never tried to pass," Guy reminisces. "Folks thought I was white and I didn't enlighten them. Whenever our carnival played, my dad and mother and I always bought enough tickets for my childhood friends.

"I had to start all over again," he stated Tuesday night while preparing to go on at the Plantation.

"When they produced Langston Hughes' 'Mulatto,' I thought my long awaited chance had come. Dick Huey told me the show called for a mulatto in the lead and I rushed down to make an audition. However, it happened that the play called for the son to choke his white father to death. Since it would not do for a real Negro to be on the stage killing a white man, the part was given to Lem Janey, a white boy. Sure, I was disappointed."

Was in "Blackbirds." Guy's first break in the Negro field came in his recitals and his first show job was the Lew Leslie's 1928 "Blackbirds" when he played the juvenile lead. He had met Donald Heywood, a personal friend, some time before that and Heywood wrote several songs for him, which he featured. Guy detests cabaret work, but he has to eat. He is married to Clara Bruce, sister of Roscoe Bruce, Jr., and has two sons, Barrington Guy Jr., 11, and Bruce Guy, 5. His mother and father are living a retired life on an estate in Prince George county, Maryland, where with Barrington's brother Trevanion, 32, and an adopted brother, Jules, 28, Mrs. Guy once owned a chain of candy stores in the colored section of Washington.

E. Azalia Hackley
(1867–1922)

Emma Azalia Hackley, soprano, was born on June 29, 1967, in Murfreesboro, Tennessee. After her family moved to Detroit in 1870 she studied piano, voice and violin. Her mother, a music teacher, was her first teacher. As a young girl in Detroit, Hackley joined the Detroit Musical

Society and was quite active locally, giving recitals and playing the piano in dance orchestras. She married in 1894 and settled in Denver, Colorado. While in Denver she attended the University of Denver, where she received a Bachelor of Music degree in 1900. In 1901 she gave her recital debut in Denver, toured the Middle West, and eventually settled in Philadelphia, Pennsylvania. In Philadelphia she was the music director of the Episcopal Church of

Portrait of Azalia Hackley. Courtesy of the E. Azalia Hackley Collection, Detroit Public Library.

the Crucifixion. She also organized the People's Chorus, which consisted of one hundred singers, in 1904. The following year she gave her Philadelphia recital debut. Hackley then went to Paris for a year, where she studied with Jean de Reszke. When she returned to Philadelphia she gave her second major recital in that area.

An interesting aspect regarding the character of E. Azalia Hackley was her willingness to support young artists of color while neglecting her own career. In 1908, by giving concerts and soliciting funds, she established a fund to sponsor young artists in debut recitals, support them during their studies, and place them in teaching positions. Over the years she helped artists such as Cleota Collins, R. Nathaniel Dett, Clarence Cameron White, and Carl Diton. She settled in Chicago in 1910 and gave her farewell concert, as a singer, at Orchestra Hall in 1911. In 1912 she founded the Vocal Normal Institute, which lasted until 1916. When the institute closed she continued organizing concerts and working with community choral groups. She traveled to Japan in 1920 and toured California the following year. While on tour in California, she collapsed and retired in 1921. Emma Azalia Hackley died on December 13, 1922, in Detroit, Michigan.

SOURCES

Cuney-Hare, Maud, *Negro Musicians and Their Music* (Washington, D.C., Da Capo Press, 1936) 202–204.
De Lerma, Dominique-René, *The New Grove Dictionary of American Music* (New York: St. Martin's Press, 1986), Vol. 2, 302–303.
Lovinggood, P., *Famous Modern Negro Musicians* (New York, N.Y.: Press Forum Co., 1921/R1978), 66–68.
Southern, Eileen, *Biographical Dictionary of Afro-American and African Musicians* (Westport, CT: Greenwood Press, 1982), 153–154.

Frank Goodall Harrison

An outstanding and highly respected baritone, Frank Harrison reached the summit in academia by becoming the head of the vocal department of Talladega College in Talladega, Alabama. A native of Austin, Texas, he received his early education throughout the Austin area and later at Howard University. Additional studies followed at Columbia University. Harrison's voice instructors include Oscar Saenger, Myron Whitney, and Frank La Forge.

In addition to his academic commitments, Harrison found the time to perform in many major cities and predominantly black colleges.

SOURCES

Cuney-Hare, Maud, *Negro Musicians and Their Music* (Washington, D.C.: Da Capo Press, 1936), 381–382.

Roland Hayes
(1887–1977)

The first African American male to achieve a measure of success as a concert singer in the United States and abroad was Roland Hayes. The son of ex-slaves, he was born in Georgia and grew up in Tennessee. Arthur Calhoun was his first teacher in Chattanooga. He later studied at the historic Fisk University in Nashville. In 1911 he toured with the Fisk Jubilee

Singers. He later studied with Arthur Hubbard in Boston and with George Henschel and Amanda Ira Aldridge in London. He often arranged his own recitals, appearing across the country in many African American communities. He raised the money needed to finance his appearances at Jordan Hall and Symphony Hall in Boston. As an African American concert singer Hayes did not achieve financial success. Such was also the case for his contemporaries and those that came before him. He therefore decided to head for Europe, which was the common avenue for numerous singers stifled by racial barriers in the United States. After a slow start Hayes was well received by audiences and most critics. He sang at the Royal Chapel, Wigmore Hall and performed before the King and Queen of England. He also befriended noted musicians Edvard Grieg and Roger Quilter. Upon his return to America he was finally able to obtain a manager and enjoyed a respected reputation and successful career as a concert singer for the remainder of the first half of the twentieth century. He encouraged younger artists, such as Marian Anderson and William Warfield, and often helped financially. He received the Spingarn Medal in 1924 and later taught at Ohio State University.

SOURCES

Abdul, Raoul, *Blacks in Classical Music: A Personal History* (New York: Dodd, Mead, 1978).
Hitchcock, H. Wiley, and Sadie, Stanley, eds., *The New Grove Dictionary of American Music* (London: Macmillan, 1986).

Merritt Hedgeman

"Music Notes," *New York Amsterdam News,* **9 September 1939, 19**

Of great interest to music lovers throughout the metropolitan area is the presentation of that brilliant young tenor, Merritt Hedgeman, in concert at the Brooklyn Academy of Music, 30 Lafayette Avenue, Brooklyn, under the C.P. Stokes management on September 28.

The program will include the works of Handel, Mozart, Palloni, Massenet, Rachmaninoff, S. Coleridge Taylor, and Negro folk songs arranged by Harry Burleigh, Lawrence Brown, John Work, William C. Heilman and Merritt Hedgeman. Miss Olive Arnold will be the singer's accompanist.

Carl Diton said of Mr. Hedgeman several years ago; "He possesses an extraordinarily beautiful vocal organ. It is not too much to say that of all the young Negro tenors, Mr. Hedgeman probably shows more promise in becoming a notable musical figure than anyone who has come to our attention in recent years."

Mr. Hedgeman has studied with capable teachers in Boston and New York and has attained a great deal of popularity with student groups.

Helen Holiday
(ca. 1895–1986)

Helen Holiday gave numerous concert and opera performances throughout the 1920s and '30s. The soprano sang the title role in Verdi's *Aida* at the Metropolitan Theatre in Boston. Fabrien Sevitsky conducted the performance. She died in Boston, Massachusetts, on March 20, 1986.

SOURCES

Obituary: *The Black Perspective in Music*, Vol. 14, No. 3, 324z.

Charles Holland
(1909 – 1987)

Now Charles was one of the people who went to Europe and had a tremendous career, but was never able to make too much in-roads here. I met him in his later years. The same impressario that I go to the West Coast for, Isaiah Williams brought him over for a series of concerts. He must've been in his seventies then and just sounded glorious still, even then. You know with tenors, by the time you get into seventy, you learn that belting thing that you just let go. But he still had a lot of energy as opposed to Roland Hayes, who had the mellow tenor, easy thing. But Holland, I understand, had a big sound, which lasted of course until he died.

— *William Warfield, April 21, 1994*

Charles Holland, tenor, was born in Norfolk, Virginia, on December

27, 1909. He began studying voice at the age of fourteen. May Hamaker
Henley was his first voice teacher. In the 1930s he sang on radio programs
and throughout the nightclub circuit as a jazz singer. During this era of
jazz history he sang with such jazz giants as Fletcher Henderson and Benny
Carter. He appeared in Marc Connelly's stage drama *Green Pastures* and
appeared in the 1941 film *Hullabaloo*. He toured with the renowned Hall
Johnson Choir as tenor soloist during the 1930s. Eventually he settled in
Hollywood and studied with Georges Le Pyre. His next stop was New
York, where he studied with Clyde Burrows. While in New York he made
his Town Hall debut in October of 1940. He also performed in *Run Little
Chillun*' by Hall Johnson, *Four Saints in Three Acts* by Virgil Thompson,
and sang a leading role in Marc Blitzstein's *Airborne Symphony* in 1945.
In 1949 Holland settled in France. His European operatic debut came in
1954 at the Paris opera in *The Magic Flute* by Mozart. In 1955 he became
the first African American singer to appear with the historic Opera
Comique. As the years passed he sang Verdi's *Otello* in London, and roles
with the Nederlandshe Opera in Amsterdam, the Netherlands, and the
Norske Opera Oslo, Norway. Holland also sang in Italy, Switzerland, Scan-
dinavia, Australia, New Zealand, and Canada. In 1982, at the age of 73,
Charles Holland made his Carnegie Hall debut in New York. He died in
Amsterdam, the Netherlands, around November of 1987.

SOURCES

Jahant, Charles, *The New Grove Dictionary of American Music* (New York: St. Mar-
  tin's Press, 1986), Vol. 2, 410.
Obituary: *The Black Perspective in Music*, Vol. 15, No. 2, 224.
Southern, Eileen, *Biographical Dictionary of Afro-American and African Musicians*
  (Westport, CT: Greenwood Press, 1982), 182.

"Charles Holland, Negro Tenor, Makes First Appearance," *Musical America,* 10 November 1940, 22

Charles Holland, Negro tenor, who has sung frequently over the air, been
a member of the Hall Johnson Choir, and who will shortly appear in a
film drama, gave his first solo recital in the Town Hall on the evening of
Oct. 28.

Mr. Holland disclosed a voice of charming and appealing quality, which
was, in the main, well produced. In songs and arias within his scope, his
singing was both agreeable and satisfactory. When he wandered beyond
his province, as in 'Il mio Tesoro' from 'Don Giovanni' and 'Vesti la
Guibba,' from 'Pagliacci,' the latter given as encore, the effect was less
striking. The Aubade from 'Le Roi d'Ys' was charmingly sung, so also the

'Flower Song' from 'Carmen.' Among his Lieder, Brahms's 'An eine Aeol-sharfe' was excellent, and Duparc's 'Chanson Triste' was well given.

The Hyers Sisters

Anna Madah (soprano) and Emma Louise (contralto) began study-ing voice and piano at ages seven and nine in Sacramento, California, where they were born. Their father, Sam B. Hyers, managed them. On April 22, 1867, they made their public debut concert at the Metropolitan Theatre in Sacramento. The concert was a major success. As a result, Sam Hyers took his daughters on a concert tour of the eastern United States. On August 12, 1871, the Hyers sisters gave their first professional concert at the Salt Lake Theatre in Salt Lake City. By the time the sisters arrived in Chicago, word had reached the windy city that they were musical prodi-gies to be reckoned with. Anna was compared to Jenny Lind and Emma was praised for her deep rich voice. Later Sam Hyers enlarged the troupe by enlisting the talents of Wallace King, tenor, and John Luca, baritone. They performed throughout New York State and eventually landed in Boston, Massachusetts. Their performances also took them to Rhode Island and Connecticut. In 1872 P.S. Gilmore invited the sisters to sing at the World Peace Jubilee in Boston. They remained there and in 1875 per-formed regularly at Boston Theatre. In 1876 Sam Hyers enlarged the troupe once again, adding drama and musical comedy to their repertoire. The dramatic play "Out of Bondage," and the musical "Blackville Twins" and "Colored Aristocracy" were some of their productions. Emma died before 1900. Anna retired in 1902 after appearing with John H. Isham's Oriental American Company.

SOURCES

Curey-Hare, Maude, *Negro Musicians and Their Music* (Washington, D.C.: Da Capo Press, 1936), 215–218.
Sampson, Henry T., *The New Grove Dictionary of American Music* (New York: St. Martin's Press, 1986), Vol. 2, 445–446.

Caterina Jarboro
(1903–1986)

I never got to know her, but she was quite big, well known all over.

— *William Warfield, April 21, 1994*

Soprano Caterina Jarboro (originally Caterina Yarborough) was the first African American female singer to have a leading role with a white opera company in the United States. She created this sensation on July 22, 1933, singing the title role of Verdi's *Aida* with the Chicago Civic Opera Company. Alfredo Salmaggi conducted. She was born in Wilmington, North Carolina, on July 24, 1903. Around 1916 she went to New York to continue her musical growth. In the early 1920s she sang in Broadway musicals, including *Shuffle Along* by Eubie Blake and Noble Sissle (1921), and *Runnin' Wild* (1923) by James P. Johnson. In 1926 she went to Paris. In 1928 she went to Italy to study with Nino Campinno. In May of 1930 she made her operatic debut as *Aida* at the Puccini Theatre in Milan. She returned to the United States in 1932 and made her American operatic debut with the Chicago Civic Opera the following year as *Aida* once again. In the fall of 1933 she sang the role of Selika in *L'Africaine* by Meyerbeer at

Portrait of Caterina Jarboro. Photographs and Prints Division, Schomburg Center for Research in Black Culture, The New York Public Library, Astor, Lenox and Tilden Foundations.

the Hippodrome Theatre in New York. Her career in the United States failed to develop as she had hoped. As a result, she returned to Europe in 1937 and settled in Brussels, Belgium. She toured Europe widely. However, due to the outbreak of war, she returned to the United States in 1941. She finally settled in New York City and retired in 1955. Caterina Jarboro died there on August 13, 1986.

SOURCES

Curey-Harc, Maude, *Negro Musicians and Their Music* (Washington, D.C.: Da Capo Press, 1936) 362–364.
Obituary: *The Black Perspective in Music,* Vol. 114, No. 3, 342.
Southern, Eileen, *Biographical Dictionary of Afro-American and African Musicians* (Westport, CT: Greenwood Press, 1982), 201.

"Caterina Jarboro, Soprano. Oscar Kosches, accompanist. Carnegie Hall Feb. 6 evening," *Musical America,* 10 March 1944, 12

Mme. Jarboro demonstrated her popularity by drawing an almost capacity audience to Carnegie Hall, no mean feat in itself. The program was an excellent one, in the main, and contained a number of eminently worthwhile songs unfamiliar to the present reviewer.

The singer tempted fate by beginning with the exceedingly difficult Handel work, but triumphed with it. In fact, it was one of the best pieces of singing of the evening, and by far the best of the first group. In the French group the singer got into her stride and practically all of the songs were well done, especially the "Chanson Romaine." In the final group, the first and the last were the best sung. The "Sigurd" excerpt is not particularly impressive music but it was well given.

Mme. Jarboro has what is unquestionably one of the finest soprano voices of the time. That she gets out of it all the beauty possible cannot, unfortunately, be said. There is a dry, nasal patch from about D to G above that mars consistently songs entering this terrain. The high voice is well produced in both forte and piano passages. Her breathing is firm and her pitch generally good.

On the emotional side, Mme. Jarboro either does not delve sufficiently into the depths of her songs, or she is ill-advised, for she frequently uses a bright, glittering tone where the sentiment of the song is either dark or somber. This happened a number of times.

At best, her singing was arresting on account of its vitality, its volume and general seriousness. At the other extreme, one wished it were a shade better so that it might have been entirely excellent.

Thomas Henry Johnson

Tenor Thomas Henry Johnson was born in Birmingham, Alabama. After graduating from Morehouse College he continued his vocal training at the New England Conservatory of Music. Jordan Hall, of Boston, was the site of his debut recital. Concert tours and appearances in theatrical productions across the United States followed.

SOURCES

Cuney-Hare, Maude, *Negro Musicians and Their Music* (Washington, D.C.: Da Capo Press, 1936), 380.

Matilda Sissieretta Jones
(1869–1933)

Soprano M. Sissieretta Jones was born on January 5, 1869, in Portsmouth, Virginia. Her maiden name was Matilda S. Joyner. In the mid–1870s her family moved to Providence, Rhode Island. There she began her formal music education. She studied with Ada Lacombe at the Providence Academy of Music. During the 1880s she studied singing at the New England Conservatory and worked privately with Luisa Capianni and Madame Scongia of London, England. As a young woman she developed a remarkable dramatic soprano voice. Her first major appearance came on April 5, 1888, at Steinway Hall in New York. It was a James Bergen Star Concert Production, which also featured Flora Batson. She debuted at the Academy of Music in Philadelphia, Pennsylvania, a month later. As a member of the Tennessee Concert Company, she toured the West Indies during the summer of 1888. She was originally dubbed "Black Patti" by the managers of the Metropolitan Opera, Abbey Schoeffel, and Grau. However, it was her West Indies tour that gave her the public acclaim she so richly deserved, thus giving her title a new meaning that would last for the remainder of her career. She continued concertizing and returned to the West Indies in 1890. This time she went with the Star Tennessee Jubilee Singers. The African American impresario Florence Williams managed the ensemble.

Portrait of M. Sissieretta Jones, known as "the Black Patti." Photographs and Prints Division, Schomburg Center for Research in Black Culture, The New York Public Library, Astor, Lenox and Tilden Foundations.

In 1892 she sang at the White House at the invitation of President Benjamin Harrison. From April 26 to 29, 1892, she was the featured singer for the "Grand Negro Jubilee" at Madison Square Garden in New York. She sang at the Pittsburgh Exposition and the Chicago World's Fair in 1893. She and her white manager, James B. Pond, had a legal battle when she tried to negotiate a contract with better terms. By 1894 she had successfully parted with Pond and signed with Ednorah Nahor, an African American impresario. Nahor also managed Rachel Walker. Jones signed with the Damrosch Orchestra Company in the fall of 1894, touring extensively abroad and across the United States. She changed her career abruptly in 1896 by becoming the leading soprano in a newly formed vaudeville company, Black Patti's Troubadours. The white proprieters, Voelckel and Nolan, managed the company. The company toured internationally until 1915. Changes in public taste brought the company's run to a close. Jones intended to retire at this time, but returned to the stage in the fall of 1915 as soloist at the Grand Theater in Chicago, Illinois, and at the historic Lafayette Theater in Harlem. She also entertained the African American soldiers during World War I. Sissieretta Jones was one of the most celebrated African American singers of the late nineteenth century. Many admired the richness and dramatic power of her soprano voice. She was admired greatly for her diction and her high level of musicianship. Matilda Sissieretta Jones died in Providence, Rhode Island, on June 24, 1933.

Sources

Cuney-Hare, Maud, *Negro Musicians and Their Music* (Washington, D.C.: Da Capo Press, 1936), 230–231.

Southern, Eileen, *Biographical Dictionary of Afro-American and African Musicians* (Westport, CT: Greenwood Press, 1982), 217–218.

Wright, Josephine, *New Grove Dictionary of American Music* (New York: St. Martin's Press, 1986), Vol. 2, 595.

New York Age, 12 May 1888

Philadelphia, 8 May.— Last Thursday night the Academy of Music held an audience of nearly 3,000 persons. It was the occasion of another famous Bergen concert. Miss Flora Batson was as usual the great attraction and although only down on the bill for three numbers, had to sing eleven times to satisfy the audience. Mrs. M. S. Jones of Providence appeared here on that occasion, for the first time, and created a marked impression. Her voice is sweet, sympathetic and clear, and her enunciation a positive charm. She was recalled after each number.

New York Age, 4 August 1888

A rehearsal was held at Wallack's Theatre Wednesday afternoon by a company of colored singers who sailed Thursday morning on the steamer Athos for Jamaica. They will also make a tour through the West Indies, the Windward Islands and the Spanish Main. Mrs. Matilda Jones, a young lady of 20 years, and Mr. W. H. Pierce of Providence will be the stars of the affair. Mrs. Jones is called the "Black Patti" by such men as Abbey, Schoeffel and Grau (managers of the Metropolitan opera), who should be competent to judge such matters. Mr. Pierce is said to be one of the finest tenors in the country. The organization (called the Tennessee Concert Company) is under the management of James R. Smith, while C.H. Matthews will remain to look after the bank account. It is one of the most promising enterprises that has ever been planned for colored artists.

The Freeman, 20 April 1889

Miss Florence Williams, in interviewing Mr. James R. Smith, was informed by him concerning the Tennessee Concert Company, that the company had disbanded owing to a misunderstanding, that the singers have become swell-headed and did not wish to accord him any credit whatever for his share in bringing them before the world. The company, having gained recognition as singers under his management, then rebelled against him and thus broke their contract. Miss Kate Johnson and Mr. Lewis Brown claim that the contract was not broken by any action of the company, but by the manager and that the company had been duped by the manager. They claimed that all their expenses were to be paid by Smith, which he failed to do. Mr. Smith should remember that some of his artists had established a reputation before he had even proposed a trip to the West Indies for them ...

The Freeman, 20 April 1889

Last week, at Dockstader's Theatre, Broadway, New York, and a company known as the Georgia Minstrels appeared all week in good business. The troupe consisted of Mme. M. S. Jones, DeWolf Sisters, Messrs. Lew Brown, W. Owens King, Will H. Pierce, Dick Jones, Western [i.e., Weston], Lew Allen and the Excelsior Quartet.

It may be surprising to note the names of some of the artists who appeared in the Georgia Minstrels in New York last week. An actor's lot is not a happy one; up today and down tomorrow.

The Freeman, 18 May 1889

Mme. M. S. Jones, prima donna soprano, and Mr. Lewis L. Brown, baritone, have lately signed contracts for a short Southern tour under the management of B. F. Lightfoot.

[The following item was published in The Freeman *(Indianapolis) on 22 June 1889, but is inserted here because of its relevance to the preceding item. It is an excerpt from an interview of Will A. Pierce, "the famous silvertoned tenor" of the Tennessee Concert Company, by C. W. Anderson, contributor of a column entitled "The Stage" to* The Freeman. *Pierce described some of the experiences of the troupe on its tour of the West Indies.]*

We left New York on August 2nd on the steamer Athos; we arrived at Kingston, Jamaica, on the 10th. We opened at the Royal Theatre on Monday evening to an overcrowded house. We had the patronage of his excellency, the Honorable J. C. Robinson, governor, and Lady Robinson ... We gave sixty performances in Jamaica altogether, then we traveled through the Windward Islands, playing to packed houses, after which we crossed the Isthmus of Panama, stopping at Apsinwll, where we played a week at the celebrated Sarah Bernhardt Theatre, which was the handsomest one I have ever seen .... Then we played in Panama ... for two weeks. This is the place where Madame Jones, the prima donna of the troupe, was first styled the "Black Patti" ... Mme. Jones was a success such as has never been achieved by a colored soprano in this section. Nightly the stage was perfectly covered with floral tributes presented by the ladies; she also received seven solid gold medals during the tour....

[The interview was continued in the 29 June 1889 issue of The Freeman.]*

We then went to Colon ... to Trinidad ... to Barbados. From there we went up in the Dutch land, or what is better known as Dutch Guinea, playing a week to people who could not understand us. We went ... to St. Kitt ... We had a chorus that sang jubilee selections, besides a high class of soloists. (We were abroad) six months....

New York Age, 10 August 1889

Mme. Jones will sing at Newport, Richfield Springs and Saratoga before her departure for the West Indies.

New York Age, 17 October 1891

On Thursday evening, October 17th, a Bergen Star concert was given at the Bridge Street Church, Brooklyn .... Mrs. Flora Batson Bergen and

Mrs. Matilda S. Jones were the stars of the evening ... Mrs. Jones was greeted with applause. She has a pleasing voice, completely under control. This is her first appearance in Brooklyn. On Monday evening, Mrs. Bergen and Mrs. Jones appeared at Bethel Church, this city (i.e., Manhattan), before a large and enthusiastic audience and repeated their Brooklyn triumph ... Madame Jones's rendition of the Meyerbeer Cavatina make good her claim as an artist of high order ...

"Madame Sissieretta at White House,"
Washington Post, 25 February 1892

Mme. M. Sissieretta Jones, who possesses a voice of extraordinary compass, that has given her the title of the "Colored Patti" and medalist of the age, appeared before President Harrison, his family and guests at the Executive mansion at 10 o'clock. The selections presented were "Cavatina" by Meyerbeer; "Swanee River;" Waltz by Pattison, and "Home, Sweet Home." Professor Charles Dunger accompanied her on the piano.

"The Great Prima Donna," *Washington Bee,* 28 February 1892

Madame M. Sissieretta Jones Creates a Sensation. Washington's Best Society greets the popular Singer. She is received by the President and His Family.

Madame M. Sissieretta Jones is the name of the lady who has won a reputation of which she should feel proud, one who is an honor to the colored race!

Her first concert was given at the Metropolitan Church on M Street between 15th and 16th Streets, N.W., on last Monday evening before the largest audience that has filled that fine structure. Never before in the history of that church has there been such a crowd. This is no fancy picture; every available space was filled and dozens had to be turned away. Mr. George Martin, one of the best known citizens of Washington and who is justly styled "King of Ticket Sellers," was the manager of this concert. Too much cannot be said of the enterprise and ingenuity that he demonstrated to make the affair a success.

The concert at Ebenezer Church on Tuesday night was a success in every particular. Standing room could not be obtained.

On Monday evening Madame Jones was greeted by a large audience in Lannon's Opera House, Alexandria, Virginia. A large number of white citizens turned out.

On Wednesday morning Madame Jones, accompanied by her husband and Professor Charles Dunger, sang before the President and his family. A handsome souvenir in the form of an invitation was prepared by the BEE ...

The receptions that were accorded Madame Jones were well earned when they left Thursday for Baltimore, Maryland.

"A Wonderful Performance," *New York Herald,* 27 April 1892

Over five thousand persons assembled in Congress Park last evening to hear Mrs. Sissieretta Jones, the "Black Patti," sing. The concert was held in the lake pavilion, which was completely surrounded by a cultured throng. After three selections by the orchestra, Mrs. Jones appeared and sang an aria from "Robert le Diable" and in response to a rousing encore gave "Maggie, the Cows Are in the Clover," a third selection was demanded and gracefully given before she was allowed to retire. Later in the evening she sang Gilli's "Farfella" with much musical expression, which secured two encores, which were responded to. They were "The Song of the Bobolink" and "Swanee River." Her crowning success of the evening was given at the close of the programme, Gounod's "Ave Maria" with obligato by Mr. Kilian. Although there were repeated calls for an encore, she did not respond.

Mrs. Jones possesses a beautiful voice, which has been well trained. There is neither brass in her notes nor thickness in her phrasing. Her enunciation is also perfect. The exquisite crispness with which she executes complicated scales in rapid time delighted all. Withal she sings intelligently without affectation, and with much feeling.

It is understood that she may give a second concert in the park at an early date.

"The Black Patti and a Cakewalk. Five Thousand Persons Witness a Novel Entertainment at Madison Square Garden. Applause for Mme. Jones," *Saratoga Union,* 6 August 1892 (reprinted in the *Washington Bee* 3 October 1892)

She sang the Swanee River and Selections from Grand Operas and Wasn't a Bit Nervous.

There was a study in black and white at the Madison Square Garden last night. About three-fourths of the scene, though, was in white. The big garden had been prepared for a rather unique entertainment in which the "Black Patti," heralded as "the greatest singer of her race," a lot of oddities, musical and otherwise, all colored, and Levy's American Band took part.

About five thousand persons were in the Garden at nine o'clock. The boxes were well filled, as were the arena seats, by people whom one would not often see at a cakewalk. Many of the ladies wore dazzling toilets, and evening dress was general among the men.

The last cakewalk at the Garden drew a crowd, but was generally regarded as "fake." Shrewd people believed, however, that there was money in a "high toned" cake walk, with other "colored" attractions thrown in, and the show last night was the result.

After the band, an alleged Alabama quartet, a double quintet of banjos and a really meritorious "Jubilee Chorus," the audience was regaled with a Southern shuffle executed by three colored damsels. Four Negroes then indulged in a "Battle Royal," or "Hit a Head When You See It." This was a free fight with soft gloves and caused amusement.

The Black Patti. When Mme. Sissieretta Jones, the "Black Patti," walked up the steps to the platform in the center of the great amphitheatre, her breast was covered with medals and she was smiling broadly. She is of Dianesque proportions, very black, but pleasing features. She was perfectly self possessed. She began the cavatina from Meyerbeer's opera, "Robert le Diable." After the first few notes the audience saw that the songstress had a remarkably strong voice, which she used with discretion.

Her effort was loudly applauded, as was her first encore, the familiar "Way Down Upon the Swanee River," which she sang in excellent taste. Recalled again, she sang "The Cows Are in the Clover" very effectively, her upper notes being especially sweet. She received an ovation.

I saw in the audience during the evening, Mr. Charles F. Chatterhorn, Mr. Appey's right hand man, whose special duty it is to look after the real Adelina Patti and talk French to her. Mr. Chatterton said to me: "This colored woman is certainly a very good natural singer, and while I should hardly feel like comparing her voice with Mme. Patti's, I find her negro dialect much better, as shown in her rendering of the "Swanee River."

Born in Virginia. I talked with the "Black Patti" in her dressing room after she had sung. She said she had not been at all nervous and found the acoustic properties of the Garden superb. She speaks of herself as a Providence girl although born in Virginia. She studied music in Boston. The last time she sang in New York was when Mr. Fred Douglass lectured at Cooper Union. She is living at the Hotel Venus, in West Seventeenth Street. She talks well, though inclined to be a bit diffident.

After a brief intermission at ten o'clock there was "buck" dancing, a "buzzard lope dance," more jubilee and more of Levy's Band. Then came the inevitable skirt dance, with colored performers, after which the "Black Patti" sang again, her selections being a farfella, "Valse Chantee" and the song "Sempre Libera" from Verdi's "La Traviata."

Then came the cakewalk, in which there were about fifty very earnest and irresistibly comical contestants. They were still walking after midnight and no one had taken the cake.

The same program will be given at the Garden tonight and tomorrow night.

"Hundreds Turned Away," *Washington Bee,* 27 August 1892

Every seat taken, tickets refused to three or four hundred people, and all standing room occupied were the state of affairs at the first Levy concert at the Auditorium. Outside the big building, the streets and sidewalks held an audience almost as large as that gathered inside. It was the largest and most enthusiastic crowd that Asbury Park ever saw in a similar entertainment. Levy is the king of cornetists and is as lively as twenty years ago. As a leader he equals Gilmore or Coppa. The selections were popular and triple and quadruple encores were insisted upon.

Madame Jones was in fine voice, and her rendering of the most difficult compositions was an easy task. The original Patti has no mean rival in her dusky competitor.

"*Black Patti* Sings to a Delighted Audience," *Cleveland Gazette,* 1 April 1893

Dayton, Ohio. — A large audience assembled at Association Hall last Wednesday evening to hear the celebrated "Black Patti." The circumstances under which the concert was given was very mystifying, but the audience nevertheless was greatly delighted, as she sang herself into the hearts of her hearers. She renders with ease some of the highest class of music as well as her simple ballads and Scotch melodies. She was assisted by Prof. Arthur Cavendish, tenor soloist; Miss Julia Galloway and Mr. Paul Lawrence Dunbar, readers.

"Lectured the Black Patti," *New York Times,* 27 June 1893

Judge McAdams Says She is Ungrateful to Major Pond — Must Sing for Him Alone

Sissieretta Jones, the "Black Patti," got a severe lecture yesterday from Judge McAdam of the Superior Court on the evils of ingratitude. Incidentally, she was enjoined from singing under any other management than that of Major James B. Pond.

On June 8, 1892, the Major made a contract for the "Black Patti" for a year. He was to pay her $150 per week, furnish all accommodations for her, and pay all traveling expenses. Some time ago the Major and his colored star disagreed, and they have been contending in the courts for several months over a clause in the contract which gave the manager the privilege of re-engaging the singer for an additional two years under the same terms provided for the first year's work.

The "Black Patti" wanted to engage in business for herself, and Major Pond applied to Judge McAdam for an injunction. In granting the motion, the court said yesterday of Sissieretta: "She feels now as if she could get along without her benefactor, and she has thrown down the ladder on which she ascended to the position she now enjoys. Every sense of gratitude requires her to be loyal to the Manager who furnished her with the opportunity for greatness, and every principle of equity requires her to perform her engagements according to the spirit and intent of the contract. Talent is of little value without opportunity, and history records on its brightest pages the names of many who would have died in obscurity but for opportunity."

"Worlds Fair Music. Rendered by Madame Selika, the Black Patti, Mr. Woodward and Madame Pinto. The *Gazette*'s Critic Writes Interestingly of Them From a Musical Standpoint — Their Strong and Weak Points — Also Their Success in the Windy City Special to the Gazette," *Cleveland Gazette,* Walt B. Hayson, 21 October 1893

Chicago, Ill — On September 25 it was advertised through the World's fair grounds that the "Black Patti" would sing in the women's building in the afternoon. One hour before the time of her appearance the large building was literally packed, so eager were both American and foreigner to hear the famous singer. Nor were their expectations disappointed, if we may judge from the ovation, which followed her song, "Ocean, Thou Mighty Monster." Public opinion, in accord with the best musical criticism, proclaims her the greatest coming singer. She draws her selections from every source, but her favorite seems to be "Fleur des Alps," although she sings with good effect "Robert le Diable," both songs being well adapted to bring out the quality and phenomenal range of her voice. When compared with Selika, the tones of her upper register are thinner, but this defect is entirely compensated for by her fuller and deeper tones of the lower. Madame Jones's voice is always musical; there is present, too, that spirit, that musical taste and insight, that is found only in the born artist. One hears such mellow, sweet, rich tones that while she sings he sits enraptured and as the last tone dies away involuntarily bursts out into applause. She has pleased us often by responding to encores with "Swanee River." May she ever honor that most soulful American folk song.

Cleveland Gazette, 21 October 1893

Pittsburgh and Allegheny, Pa.— ...Madame Jones, the "Black Patti," returns to the Exposition again this week. Of all the artists, Scalchi Materna, Campanin, Brooks,' Gilmore's and other celebrated New York Bands, and other attractions (white) at the Pittsburgh Exposition, none have drawn such crowds as Madame Jones, and none are secured twice in a season by the Exposition managers.

"Dvorak Leads for the Fund. National Conservatory Concert Contributes Largely to the Herald's Charity. A Promising Child Pianist *Old Folks at Home* Heard for First Time with Dr. Dvorak's Orchestration Costly Baton for Dvorak Honor to Mrs. Jeanette M. Thurber, to Dr. Antonin Dvorak and the students of the National Conservatory of Music!" *New York Herald,* 24 January 1894

> Mme. Sissieretta Jones, the "Black Patti," the only soloist not a pupil at the Conservatory, sang the soprano solo in the "Inflammatus," from Rossini's "Stabat Mater," the chorus being sung by the colored male choir of St. Phillip's Church, under the direction of Mr. Edward B. Kinney, the organist and choirmaster of the church and a pupil in Dr. Dvorak's composition class. Mme. Jones was an enormous success with the audience. To those who heard her for the first time she came in the light of a revelation, singing high C's with as little apparent effort as her namesake, the white Patti. It was impossible to refuse the demand for and encore, so Mme. Jones responded with the "Robert, toi que j'aime," in which she was accompanied by her pianist, Miss Wilson.

Cleveland Gazette, 22 December 1894

> Springfield, O.—Madame Sissieretta, the "Black Patti," sang at Black's opera house last Wednesday evening under the auspices of the G.A.R. Madame Jones was supported by a good organization of vocal artists.

> Dayton, O.—"The 'Black Patti' Here, Also." Black Patti sang at the Grand Opera House Thursday evening.

"Mme. Sissieretta Jones," *Berliner Frembenblatt,* 20 February 1895

> The World's greatest Afro-American songstress, now traveling in Europe, takes the land of William and Bismark by storm. See comment of German press below:
> Miss Sissieretta [sic] Jones, known in America as the "Black Patti" made her first appearance in the Wintergarten yesterday. The singer's pleasant delicately bronzed face protests against the first part of this name, but the enthusiastic applause her singing called forth proved the epithet to be true at least. The first number, Gounod's "Valse Arietta," showed ability to manage the most difficult florid music. "The Last Rose of Summer" showed her decided talent for expression of sentiment. Her voice is clear and pure up to the highest tones. The admiration awakened by the singer was not wholly due to her interesting appearance and to her tasteful costume, but was in great part a tribute to her really remarkable ability.

Norddeutsche Allgemeine Zeitung. The program of the Wintergarten
has been enriched by the acquisition of the American singer, Miss
Sissieretta Jones, whose rich flexible voice and admirable musical delivery have earned for her the name of the "Black Patti." The comparison
is not a bad one, for we have here to do with a singer, who not only
attracts our interest because of her nationality, but whose full sweet voice
charms her hearers at once. The impression made upon the audience was
so favorable that instead of the one song announced, Miss Jones was
obliged to sing five. Beside the fine gifts with which nature has endowed
her, Miss Jones has enjoyed a most excellent musical schooling. This is
shown in the easy, natural manner of her singing, there is no seeking for
effect, only the endeavor to render music and text their true effect. Her
voice has power and fire, and the florid passages remind one of the rapid
flow of a mountain brook. The Wintergarten has won a fine representation of the act of bel canto in the "Black Patti," and her songs bring an
element of true art into the program of this country.

Kreuz-Zeitung. Miss Sissieretta Jones, the true "Black Patti" a singer of
repute in America, made her first appearance in the Wintergarten yesterday. The lady is a mulatto of pleasing appearance, and soon won the
hearty applause of the large audience. Miss Jones possesses great natural
gifts, which have been well trained. Her singing shows musical ability and
her delivery is excellent. She sang the "Valse Ariette," which Gounod
composed for Adelina Patti. Her other numbers were two American compositions and the "Last Rose of Summer."

Post. Miss Sissieretta Jones, known in her American home as the "Black
Patti" made her debut in the Wintergarten last evening. Only half the
name fits but fortunately the better half. "Patti," we may rightly call her,
although we protest against the adjective "Black." Miss Jones is a young
woman of most pleasing appearance and only her full lips and delicate
brown tint of her complexion betray her mulatto blood. The only thing
"black" about her is the beautiful shining hair. Miss Jones is an artist who
can stand the test of severest musical criticism. Her well-trained voice is
of great range and fine carrying power. Her technical ability is admirable,
she executes the most difficult florid passages with perfect ease, and the
good taste of her delivery shows natural talent developed by careful and
well directed study. A certain sharpness in the upper tones may have been
the fault of the hall. Miss Jones is in short, a singer, who well deserves
the applause, which greeted her every number.

Borsen-Courier. She is in Europe for the first time, Miss Sissieretta
Jones, or the "Black Patti" as she is called in America. The singer must
have seen many things to interest and impress her since her landing from
the "Ems," and she herself has made a remarkable impression on this, her
first appearance before a German audience. Our trans-atlantic cousins

have not exaggerated in comparing their countrywoman with Patti, but the adjective "black" seems to us unnecessarily impolite. Miss Jones is evidently of Negro blood, but not alone of Negro blood. She is a mulatto of bronzed complexion and pleasant expressive features, with full lips and high forehead and the bearing of a lady, even to the choice of her costume. The American singer wore a tasteful gown of salmon pink silk covered with jet trimmings. She wore little jewelry; the ensemble was in excellent taste. Miss Jones possesses natural gifts, which have been carefully trained. This alone would secure her sucess. And she possesses as well that which no schooling can give, musical understanding and warm feeling. The colored artist sings with absolute purity and perfect correctness, her high notes are of fine power, the deeper tones rich and full, and her management of rapid passages remarkable. She began with the "Valse Ariette," composed by Gounod for Adelina Patti, sang then two American songs and the "Last Rose of Summer," apparently to allow the German audience opportunity for comparison. It turned out entirely to her favor, and the applause which greeted the close of each number was worthy tribute to a talent which is quite independent of color or nationality, a talent worthy of admiration for its own sake alone, and which can well appeal to an intelligent audience. The "Black Patti" will soon see that her worth is recognized in Berlin, and the manager of the Wintergarten deserved all thanks for offering us the opportunity of hearing this transatlantic star.

The [Indianapolis] Freeman, 4 May 1895

What one of Berlin's chief musical critics says of Mme. Sissieretta Jones— "Scarcely had the great Adelina Patti ceased to charm her hearers in the Philharmonic, before Messrs. Dorn and Baron, managers of the Wintergarten had found us another Queen of Song."

"Black Patti and Miss Fowler," Savannah Tribune, 9 May 1896

The Moody Tabernacle in Atlanta contained some three thousand people last week to listen to "Black Patti" (Mme. Sissieretta Jones), the famous colored prima donna, supported by other talent. Patti was in good condition and pleased her audience immensely in singing an Aria from *Traviata* and "Incantatrice" and as encores rendered "Comin' thro the Rye," the "Cows are in the Corn," and "Swanee River."

The program was excellently carried out by the local talent acquitting themselves finely, but it was left to Savannah's charming and brilliant young favorite Miss Georgia A. Fowler to divide the honors with the "queen of song."

"Black Patti's Troubadours," *The Colored American* (Washington, D.C.), 14 May 1898

Black Patti (Mme. Sissieretta Jones), who for several years past has won the highest lyric honors on the concert stage, and who is endowed with a marvelous voice, sweet in quality and of extensive range, has abandoned the concert stage in favor of comedy, vaudeville and opera. This great singer is the star of "The Black Patti's Troubadours," an organization comprising fifty celebrated artists and which is said to be the most imposing aggregation of colored performers ever organized. The stage entertainment offered by this company is attractive, sensational and novel. It embraces comedy, burlesque, ballet, vaudeville and opera presented with appropriate scenery, elegant and costly costumes and all the necessary stage surroundings requisite for a perfect artistic performance.

"At Jolly Coney Island" is a title of a merry and laugh-provoking skit, which serves as a curtain raiser and vehicle to give free rein to the company's comedy and singing forces. This travesty is followed by a great vaudeville olio and selections from the various standard grand and comic operas. In the operatic oli Black Patti has great opportunities to display her wonderful voice. She sustains the principal roles of The Grand Duchess, Carmen, Bohemian Girl, Trovatore, Lucia, Maritana, Tar and Tartar, and The Daughter of the Regiment. The rendition which she and the entire company give of this repertorical opera selections is said to be incomparably grand. Not only is the solo singing of the highest order, but also the choruses are rendered with a spirit and musical finish, which never fail to excite genuine enthusiasm. The work of Black Patti and the company has received the highest marks of public approval, and the forthcoming performances here will doubtless be highly appreciated. The Troubadours will be at the Grand Opera House for one week, beginning Monday evening, May 16.

The Colored American (Washington, D.C.), 9 July 1898

Mme. Sissieretta Jones (Black Patti) is in great demand for special summer engagements, but she is loath to abandon her plans for perfect rest during the heated term. She will open her third starring season in September at the head of the Black Patti's Troubadours, under the management of Voelckel and Nolan. Mme. Jones commands the handsome salary of $500 per week, and is one of the best drawing cards on the road.

The Colored American, 20 May 1899

"Black Patti" and her Troubadours will go to the Paris Exposition. They are already brushing up on their "parlez vous Francais," preparatory toward invading the land of the Napoleons and grape juice.

**"The *Black Patti* one of the world's most tuneful cantatrices.
A singer of high-class music!" *The [Indianapolis] Freeman,*
27 December 1902**

In her selections from the Grand Opera of Martha she rivals the inter-
preters of the intermezzo from Mascagni's Cavalieria Rusticana.

Perhaps the pre-eminently distinguished singer before the footlights
today is Sissieretta Jones, commonly referred to as "Black Patti" whose
voice and figure in no mean reference have been likened unto those of
the diva who has seemingly taken up permanent residence and a retired
life at Craig-y-Nos across the briny deep (a reference to Adelina Patti).

Sissieretta Jones has gone on uninterruptedly in the noiseless tenor of
her way, and attained a success that comes as a private property of those
only who take good care of superior vocal organs. If we remember aright,
the first time we ever heard "Black Patti" sing was in the rooms of the
YMCA in Kansas City, Mo., about seven or eight years ago. We were then
working on a small weekly paper in Leavenworth, Kas. and paid 75 cents
out of our meager earnings to go to Kansas City to hear her sing. We went
prepared to be disappointed because we had heard so much about her
marvelous voice in the *New York Journal* and other metropolitan newspapers that we concluded she could not possibly be all that the newspapers claimed for her. We are not much given to excess or over-ripe
adulation unless the person upon whom we thrust it is worthy, and then,
perchance, we are liable to "slop-over," but in the case of Mme. Jones we
found her voice to be all that it had been represented, and more too. Since
our initiation into the mysteries of a voice of a consonant register, and
one of a ministry which is quite naturally melodious, we have on three
or four occasions been inspired to say something commendatory of it;
and in no way could we have been better pleased than when the managing editor of *The Freeman* asked us to say something under Mme. Jones's
portrait. We have watched such like, as have been given us by watches
for the emergence of Santa Claus from a soot-befuddled chimney—until
King Morpheus, with a kindly hand, has drawn the tender lids over its
dreamy eyes—and, like a child, we have been aroused or waked up to
find our sublimest hopes fulfilled. Cautious and cynical critics, such as
"Chicot," of the *New York Telegram*, and his tribe, who claim to be up
on song and songcraft claim with some degree of truth that the Negro is
not prepared for the classics in music; that he excels only in his weird
and somewhat nasal euphonies of plantation and camp meeting melodies
and such like, as have been given to us by the immortal Stephen Collins
Foster. Further along we learnedly informed by these self-same critics,
whose preponderance of cheek is sometimes overbalanced only by their
misplacement of English words and superlatively bad spelling, that the

Negro might excel in what they are delighted to term "rag-time opera." That he might excel now mark you, not that he does! But we do not care to enlarge upon so unworthy a subject as "rag-time opera." Personally, we have the highest regard for those who have dittied the words of bunglesome and sometimes suggestive stanzas to a music which is whistlingly "catch," but we should not insist on this sort of regalement.

Indeed, we submit in all candor that in Mme. Jones the Negro has an exponent of as high-grade music as can be found in any people. The Negro has the talent — is adapted to any sort of music, however seemingly arduous, and he can with as much ease as anyone else bring it out with all its inherent sweetness. That is an erroneous assertion, which teaches that the fundamental prerogative in the interpretation of high-grade music is education. It may be a fact that an educated farmer makes more advancement in the cultivation of the sod than one with only the rudimentary trimmings, but we insist that education does not obtain as to the cultivation of the voice of a singer, any more than it does to the cultivation of the violin or piano literature or the technique of a violin or piano player. As witness Jan Kubelik, whose ignorance, it is said, is excelled only by his modesty, or witness Blind Tom, who has thrilled and delighted millions thrice again.

We believe, as Mr. Dvorak, of New York, that music is an inherent quality in the Negro; he comes by music as naturally as a duck takes to water.

Comparisons are said to be odious, but by comparison we do not think Mme. Jones would suffer any with any of the grand opera soprano stars, as Mmes. Calve, Melba, Nordica, Eames, Miss Sybil Sanderson, Miss Suzanne Adams or Fraulein Fritzi Scheff. Indeed, Mme. Jones's interpretations of the selections from Martha and other standard operas place emphasis upon her capabilities as songstress. Nordica as Iseult, Eames as Aida, or Adams as Marguerite in the full operas from those names are hardly more pleasantly recalled or are more acceptable than Jones who sings the role of Martha in brief fractions. And does Sanderson sing Juliette more sweetly or more entrancingly? We would rather think not. We would as like see and hear Jones as to see and hear any one of the other notables, and the more so, perhaps, because of the fact that no advance agent is sent on ahead with a diagram advising where we may locate the register, the pliables of her voice of the staccato movement. We do not necessarily have to be "educated" to understand music — to distinguish between the good, the bad and the indifferent. We recognize it as soon as we meet it in the road, the same, as we are aware of the fact when we stub our great toe. No one need take the pains upon oneself to tell us. We feel the pains in the marrow of our bones, and we know they are there, and to speak inelegantly, when Mme. Jones "loosens up" we know she possesses the goods and is going to give us our money's worth. And we shall have no change or kick coming. She is a singer, every inch of her, with a well-modulated and distinct mezzo-soprano vocalness whose volubility is rich and thrilling. In the else serious numbers or the softer and simpler ballads Mme. Jones is a pleasing person, and with an even temperament and other admirable graces that contribute so materially to her attractions of voice, she makes a figure that is away up in rank of those whose dexterity and merit have forced them out of the ordinary file.

Ever since we heard Mme. Jones sing for the first time, seven or eight years ago, it has been our duty seemingly to say something of her singing at least once a year. Some gentlemanly managing editor, knowing how willingly we go about so pleasant duty, has always delegated it to us. Mayhap the madame will see and read these several remarks and think them sillily gushed and capable colored songstress flattering, inasmuch as they are well spiced with adjectives, but we wish right at this point in our peroration as the literature would say, to submit to the madame and her admirers that this is a habit that has grown on us— a habit that forces us to employ a multiplicity of adjectives in emphasis of a printed inspiration. But all faults must be overlooked, and the sincerity of the purpose and its attendant items be taken cognizance of.

—L. McCorker

Juanita King
(1924–1974)

Juanita King was born on March 2, 1924, in Macon, Georgia. She received her musical education from Knoxville College, Fisk University, and the Sutthin School of Music. King also sang leading roles with Mary Cardwell Dawson's National Negro Opera Company. She sang with the Baltimore Civic Opera and other professional opera companies, and appeared in Broadway musicals as well. She died on April 2, 1974, in New York.

SOURCES
Obituary: *The Black Perspective in Music,* Vol. 2, No. 2, 226.

Altonell Hines Matthews
(1905–1977)

Altonell Hines Matthews holds a special place in American music, for she sang in the original casts of two important productions during the first half of the twentieth century, *Four Saints in Three Acts* (1934) by Virgil Thomson, and *Porgy and Bess* (1935) by George Gershwin. Her husband was the acclaimed baritone Edward Matthews. She was born in Norfolk, Virginia, in 1905. Hines graduated from Livingston College and received her master's degree in Music Education from Columbia Teacher's College. At Howard University and Virginia State College she served on the voice faculty. She also performed with Eva Jessye's Radio and Concert Choir. She died in New York on August 6, 1977.

SOURCES

Obituary: *The Black Perspective in Music,* Vol. 5, No. 2, 234.

Edward Matthews
(1907–1954)

He was killed in a car accident I believe. And he was the first Jake in *Porgy and Bess*, the first one I ever saw. Excellent voice, good sound, big sound. High baritone, not low.

— *William Warfield, April 21, 1994*

Edward Matthews, baritone, created the role of Jake in the original production of George Gershwin's opera *Porgy and Bess.* He was born on August 3, 1907, in Ossining, New York. He was a product of a very musical family. His sister, Inez, was a successful mezzo-soprano concert singer, and his mother was a church soloist. In 1926 he received a Bachelor of Arts degree from Fisk University in Nashville, Tennessee. While attending that institution he sang with the Fisk Quartet and toured Europe for a year with the Fisk Jubilee Singers. In 1928 he studied with the noted Bostonian voice teacher Arthur Hubbard in Boston, Massachusetts. He made his debut at Boston's Jordan Hall in February of 1930 and debuted at New York's Town Hall in January of the following year. African American concert artist Roland Hayes sponsored Matthews' Town Hall recital. He also appeared at New York's Carnegie Hall and made several concert tours in Central and South America. In 1932 Matthews appeared as a regular member of the Major Bowes Capitol Radio Family on CBS (Columbia Broadcasting System). He remained for seven years. He created the role of St. Ignatius in the opera *Four Saints in Three Acts* by Virgil Thomson in 1934. He re-created his role as Jake in a revival of *Porgy and Bess* in 1944, and the St. Ignatius role in a 1952 revival. Matthews taught at Fisk University, Howard University in Washington, D.C., and was teaching at Virginia State College at the time of his death. He was killed in an automobile accident near Woodbridge, Virginia, on February 20, 1954. His wife, Altonell Hines Matthews, was also a singer.

SOURCES

Cuney-Hare, Maud, *Negro Musicians and Their Music* (Washington, D.C.: Da Capo Press, 1936), 381.
Obituary: *Musical America*, March 1954, 34.
Southern, Eileen, *Biographical Dictionary of Afro-American and African Musicians* (Westport, CT: Greenwood Press, 1982), 268.

Inez Matthews
(1917–)

She had a lovely, lovely, lovely sound. Gorgeous woman too! I've known her for years and when we meet it's like we just saw each other yesterday, one of those kind of things.

— *William Warfield, April 21, 1994*

Mezzo-soprano Inez Matthews was born on August 23, 1917, in Ossining, New York. Her family was a musical one. Edward, her brother, had an extensive career as an opera singer, and her mother was a church soloist. Accompanied by her sister Helen, at the piano, Matthews sang solos as a child and also sang in her father's Baptist church choir. Numbered among her teachers are Katherine Moran Douglas, Paula Novikova, and Frederick Wilkerson. Leonard DePaur served as a major influence on Matthews and her career. She toured extensively with the Leonard DePaur Singers throughout the United States and Europe.

Her Town Hall debut came in 1947. That same year she debuted at Jordan Hall in Boston, Massachusetts, and at Kimball Hall in Chicago, Illinois. Countless recitals and appearances with noted symphony orchestras soon followed. Matthews' talent also enhanced the worlds of opera and

Inez and Edward Matthews. Courtesy of the E. Azalia Hackley Collection, Detroit Public Library.

musical theater. In the years 1944 to 1946 and 1948, she sang the title role in the Broadway production of *Carmen Jones*. The role of Irina in Kurt Weill's *Lost in the Stars* came to her in 1950, and she appeared in the 1951 revival of Virgil Thomson's *Four Saints in Three Acts*. In this production her brother Edward was also featured. For the 1960 film production of George Gershwin's *Porgy and Bess* she played the role of Serena.

From 1965 to 1970 she taught at Virginia State College in Petersburg.

SOURCES

Southern, Eileen, *Biographical Dictionary of Afro-American and African Musicians* (Westport, CT: Greenwood Press, 1982), 268.

Dorothy Maynor
(1910–)

Dorothy Maynor, of course, was an idol of mine. And the first time I heard Dorothy Maynor was as a youngster. I'm about 10 years younger than she is, so I was in college at the time she was coming. Dr. Nathaniel Dett, who came to Rochester [Eastman School of Music] to get a masters degree or whatever it was, was sort of her mentor.

And so Dorothy Maynor came to Rochester and here I am, a student at the school, you know, and I have this picture. And I asked her could she sign this picture for me and she scribbled something on it. When I looked at it I just let out a *whoop* because she said *for a colleague*.

I said, "Oh my God, for a colleague. Look what she wrote. She considers me a colleague. Oh no!"

And then of course we got to know each other very well after that. And then when I've been to New York I went to her church and sang, and at the Harlem School [the Harlem School of Music founded by Dorothy Maynor] too. She's still quite a wonderful lady. There's an effervescence about her that just wears well into age.

— *William Warfield, April 21, 1994*

Dorothy Maynor, soprano, was one of the greatest African American vocal sensations of the first half of the twentieth century. She was born on September 3, 1910, in Norfolk, Virginia. Her high school and college education took place at the historic Hampton Institute in Virginia. She received a Bachelor of Science degree in 1933. While at Hampton she came under the guidance of her mentor, Dr. R. Nathaniel Dett. She later attended Westminster Choir College in Princeton, New Jersey. She went to New York in 1935 and studied with William Klamroth and John Alan

Portrait of Dorothy Maynor. Photographs and Prints Division, Schomburg Center for Research in Black Culture, The New York Public Library, Astor, Lenox and Tilden Foundations.

Haughton. At the 1939 Berkshire Festival at Tanglewood she had the opportunity to sing for the noted conductor Serge Koussevitzky. Eventually she was offered recording opportunities with Koussevitzky and the Boston Symphony Orchestra. On November 19, 1939, she made her Town Hall debut in New York. For the next two decades the soprano performed extensively in the United States, Europe, Australia, Central America, and South America. She performed with the major orchestras of the western world, recorded extensively, and appeared on radio and television. She founded the Harlem School of the Arts (1963) after retiring from the concert stage, and served as the institute's first director until 1979. Throughout her long career, Maynor sang many operatic arias, but never appeared in an opera. She did, however, record the role of Leonore in Beethoven's *Fidelio*, with Arturo Toscanini conducting. She now lives the life of a comfortable recluse with her husband, Reverend Shelby Rooks, in Virginia.

SOURCES

De Schauensee, Max, *The New Grove Dictionary of American Music* (New York: St. Martin's Press, 1986), Vol. 3, 196.

Southern, Eileen, *Biographical Dictionary of Afro-American and African Musicians* (Westport, CT: Greenwood Press, 1982), 269.

Story, Rosalyn M., "Gift of Music," *Opera News,* February 27, 1993, 16.

"Exciting Debut Made by Dorothy Maynor — Negro Soprano Creates Sensation in First New York Recital — Sings Airs by Bach, Handel, Mozart and Spontini, with Lieder and Spirituals — A Critical Estimate," by Oscar Thompson, *Musical America,* 25 November 1939, 15

Sensational in many of its aspects was the formal recital debut of Dorothy Maynor, twenty-eight-year-old Negro soprano, made in Town Hall on the evening of Sunday, Nov. 19. Because of what had been written and said about her in connection with her singing at the Boston Symphony picnic last August a sensation was expected. The audience was one of capacity size and its enthusiasm was such as to indicate that hopes — expectations might be a better word — were realized.

When Miss Maynor first came out on the platform — a short, stocky figure, attractively gowned in the color known as "blonde" — there was prodigious applause, although probably not twenty persons among those present had ever heard her sing a note. Her smile and manner were ingratiating. There was no need to win over the throng. The usual frigidity of concert halls was banished from the start. Seldom is an audience so predisposed in favor of a new artist.

With the first phrases of Bach's 'To Thee, Jehovah,' it was obvious that Miss Maynor was excited. But by the time she reached her second number, the air 'O Sleep, why dost thou leave me' from Handel's 'Semele,' her diaphragm was under control and she spun the air's long phrases with enchanting use of a rarely beautiful pianissimo. Thereafter it was this pianissimo — and the piano and mezza-voce gradations just beyond it — that supplied most of the tonal beauty of the evening. The full voice only rarely had so musical a quality.

Virtues and Flaws. At its best, Miss Maynor's singing could be compared favorably with the singing of any vocal artist before the American public. That best was by no means always present. Hence, the report of a reviewer, once it has acknowledged that Miss Maynor made a remarkable first impression, becomes the usual story of "ifs" and "buts," with high praise — high praise — on the one hand and frank reservations and even a direct warning or two on the other. As against Miss Maynor's magical spinning of soft phrases must be set the hard and driven quality of many of her full tones, particularly in the high voice, which tended to take on a razor edge. There was also some pushing of low notes. But the most serious fault was a frequent glottis stroke — particularly on the words that began with open vowels; not (as so often happens) on the initial attack, but in the middle of a phrase.

To excitement may be charged some clipped and unsteady phrase endings. For the singer proved, particularly when singing softly, that she had almost unlimited breath and that she knew how to make it last through exceptionally long phrases. She proved also that she has the singing instinct and the sensitivity necessary to give aggressive shape to the undulations of a vocal line. Her interpretations were those of an artist. But she was not altogether wise in her choice of songs. Though it evoked perhaps the most frenetic applause of the evening, her singing of 'Die Allmacht' left perhaps the most to be desired. She was spent in the final phrases, which had more of energy than tone, and at no time did she achieve the genuinely heroic. Why she should have essayed Strauss's ungrateful 'Kling,' with its mean and uninviting high C, is a mystery. Miss Maynor had the C; she hit it squarely. But it was not a seductive tone.

Two Mozart Arias. Seduction was to be found, however, in the warmth and tenderness of her singing of Schumann's 'Du bist wie eine Blume' and through much of 'Du bist die Ruh.' There can be nothing but praise for the achievement of the aria, 'Ach, ich fuehl's' from Mozart's 'Magic Flute.' There was every reason to expect, therefore, that 'Non mi dir' from the same composer's 'Don Giovanni' would be much of the same finish and appeal. But it lost its stride in the allegro and the final action was halting in its gait and strained in effect.

Miss Maynor is an essentially refined singer. The daughter of a Methodist minister of Norfolk, Va., she was graduated from Hampton Institute and toured with its chorus abroad. There is little that can be regarded as racial in her voice or in her approach to songs. Consequently her Spirituals, though exceedingly well sung, lacked the essential Negro character that some other singers of her people have given them. The beautiful mezza-voce of 'Were you there' was that which conformed exquisitely to the patrician character of 'Du bist wie eine Blume.'

Arpad Sandor's accompaniments were admirable in tone and feeling and artistic as piano playing, if sometimes not altogether advantageous for the singer, who appeared to be hurried in the 'Vestale' air and again in 'Die Allmacht.' A much-applauded encore was 'Depuis le jour' from Charpentier's 'Louise.'

"3 Headliners to Sing Here," *New York Amsterdam News,* 25 November 1939

In a period covering less than two weeks, music lovers in New York and vicinity will have the unusual opportunity of hearing Roland Hayes, Marian Anderson, and Dorothy Maynor.

Miss Maynor, the soprano who was discovered and praised by Koussevitzky at the Berkshire Festival in Massachusetts this summer, will make her New York debut at the Town Hall on Sunday night, November 19, under the management of Evans and Saiter. A product of Hampton Institute, Miss Maynor has sung with the Westminster Choir for several years and she has been abroad.

"Dorothy Maynor Is Hit at Town Hall," *New York Amsterdam News,* 15 December 1939, 2

Dorothy Maynor, the season's newest soprano, merited the undisputed right to be known as the "singer of the decade," when she made her New York debut at the Town Hall on Saturday night.

In that overflow audience in West Forty-third street were music critics, whose expressed and implied opinions often make or mar a future; musicians, who have attained the glory for which every artist hopes; multi-millionaires, whose financial backing and influence can aid her in her desire for stardom; and hundreds of commoners who enjoy spending a dollar — maybe their last one — to hear a truly fine artist.

To pick the soprano's program apart is unnecessary, since her debut was one of artistry, exhibiting a type of interpretation that is infrequently equalled and seldom surpassed. There were genuinely pure, even tones so crystal-like in their brilliance that they will be long remembered and associated with the name of Dorothy Maynor.

There was evidence of a consistent steadiness, embellished by a display of perfect control, throughout the program, except during a brief part of the vocalist's very first number. In that particular one she showed definite signs of nervousness — and who wouldn't have been nervous on such an auspicious occasion? The battery of cameras, no doubt, contributed their share of disturbing forces.

Other outstanding features possessed by Miss Maynor are flexibility, sustaining power, dramatic ability. Her pianissimo singing is divine. Gracious in manner, charming in personality, inherently sincere the concertist exhibited a vivaciousness that is seldom so evenly displayed by a young singer.

Among her best programmed numbers were Handel's "O Sleep, Why Don't Thou Leave Me?" from "Semele"; Mozart's "Ach, ich fuhl's" from "The Magic Flute" and Schubert's "Gretchen am Spinnrade," "Die Allmacht" and "Du Bist die ruh." In her top notes in dramatic passages, however, such as those occurring in "Die Allmach," the beauty of tone quality was sacrificed for interpretation.

As encores Miss Maynor offered Schubert's "Ave Maria;" an unaccompanied spiritual called "Were You There?" (or "The Crucifixion"); Strauss' "Zueignung" and an air from "Louise," which was exquisitely rendered.

Departing from the traditional, Miss Maynor sang her spirituals in Group IV of the program and used three modern compositions by Strauss in her concluding group. In the characteristic and plaintive mood, and with accompaniments that are stressed for spirituals at Hampton Institute from which Miss Maynor was graduated before she studied with the Westminister Choir in New Jersey, the artist interpreted the following: "Communion," "By and By," "Ho, Every One That Thirsts" and "I'm Seekin' for a City." One could not help but wonder, however, why she did not include at least one of Dr. R. Nathaniel Dett's numbers on her program, in that much of her study had been complete under him at Hampton.

Managed by Evans and Salter, the soprano was ably accompanied at the piano by Arpad Sandor, who is both sympathetic and retiring. Before Miss Maynor engaged her present teacher, John Alan Haughton, she studied with Wilfred Klamroth, both of this city.

Long after the unusual concert program ended on Sunday night, the enthusiastic audience begged for more of Miss Maynor's fine music. Surely, that in itself was proof that Serge Koussevitzky's discovery of this new soprano, at the Berkshire Music Festival this past summer was a stroke of luck for her. Now it is a reality that the Boston Symphony conductor's predictions for Miss Maynor are not without justifiable claim and proportions.

"Notables Hail Miss Maynor — Soprano Thrills Thousands at Debut Concert at Town Hall," *New York Amsterdam News,* 15 December 1939, 2

Not in a decade has New York heralded a new singer as it did Dorothy Maynor, Virginia-born soprano, on Sunday night at the Town Hall. Actually, there was a brilliance in setting and spirit that rivaled the opening of the Metropolitan Opera season. Everybody was anxious to hear this 28-year-old "musical find"—and she in no way disappointed her audience.

Tickets to Miss Maynor's debut were sold out long before November 19 arrived. Standees were in line hours before concert time and a goodly number of them paid handsome prices just to hear the singer. Others were turned away.

Miss Maynor's fame had preceded her by two months. Discovered by Serge Koussevitzky, celebrated conductor of the Boston Symphony, in summer at the Berkshire Music Festival in Stockbridge, Mass., she had been called by him a "native Flagstad"—and that was endorsement enough.

Late Starting. The crowd anxiously awaited the soprano to begin her program, but it was not until 8:45 that she walked on the stage. The hand-clap ovation she received then and throughout the evening literally rocked the walls of that historic hall in which hundreds of musicians of all races and nationalities have started on the road to fame.

Cameras clicked in double quick order on this night-of-nights for a brand new star. Miss Maynor, whose features, color and hair show a distinct mixture of Negro and Indian ancestry, is short and stocky. She wore a well-fitted dress of gold lame with long sleeves, overhanging puffs at each shoulder, and a slight train on the full skirt. Tiny buttons adorned the dress at the back, which modestly featured a slit form, the neckline to the waist. Her heels, it is said, were elevated three inches to giver her the desired height for a pleasing stage appearance.

"Dorothy Maynor Wins Award by Town Hall — Negro Soprano Chosen as Winner of Endowment Series by Unanimous Vote," *Musical America*, 25 March 1940, 33

By a unanimous vote, Dorothy Maynor, Negro soprano, has been selected as the winner for 1940 of the Town Hall Endowment Series Award by the Town Hall Music Committee, Walter W. Naumberg, and chairman. The award is made each season to the artist under thirty years of age that the New York music critics and the committee consider to have given the outstanding performance of the year in the Town Hall. The critics co-operate by suggesting candidates for the honor. Miss Maynor gave her New York debut recital in the hall on Nov. 19, 1939. She is the third recipient of the award.

The young soprano, who has been heard with the principal symphony orchestras in the East, as well as in recitals in various musical centres, sang the Town Hall Endowment series on Feb. 28, replacing Georges Enesco, who is detained in Europe, and had already been engaged for an appearance in the same series for January, 1941, before the award was made.

Philadelphia Record, 20 October 1945

Miss Maynor achieved enchanting singing, reaping a series of well-merited ovations. She has the magic gift of creating a mood. She has sensitive musical perceptions and sings as if she loved to sing—from the heart. Moreover, what she sings has a way of going straight to the hearts of her hearers.

Always there is a touching devotion to music. In short, Dorothy Maynor is a rare musical personality as well as an uncommonly gifted artist.

— E.H. Schloss

Philadelphia Evening Bulletin, 20 October 1945

Miss Maynor was cheered by the large audience, as well she might be, for this singer can accomplish very wonderful things with her voice, and yesterday's occasion was an excellent sample of her altogether extraordinary ability.

— M. de Schauensee

The New York Times, 21 October 1945

Miss Maynor sang … with astonishing beauty of tone and purity of style. This is the more commendable because Miss Maynor, after having at first displayed a most unusual voice and delivery, apparently underwent a period of vocal experimentation or confusion, and her technique and style began to deteriorate. On the basis of last night's demonstration, it can be said that these regressions are of the past. Like every true artist she has distances still to go, but she is now a distinguished exponent of song — of "bel canto" — and already *one of the most deserving and conspicuously gifted singers of her generation…*.

— Olin Downes

New York Journal-American, 31 October 1945

Miss Maynor gave a demonstration of vocal artistry that was perfection. Tones of flute-like beauty, each note attacked and produced with faultless control and with an economy of effort resulted in a noble and matchless interpretation.

— G. Bennett

New York World Telegram, 31 October 1945

Among the concert's treats were the topflight flutings of the gifted young soprano, Dorothy Maynor. The girl's limpid tones were heard like angels' tidings in the "Incarnatus est' from Mozart's C minor Mass. If there are lovelier soprano sounds today they should step forward and be heard or forever keep their peace.

— L. Biancolli

"Dorothy Maynor on CBS Lent Program," New York Amsterdam News, 5 March 1949, 4

Dorothy Maynor, celebrated soprano of concert and radio, will be heard on a special World Day of Prayer Program over the Columbia network, Friday, March 4, CBS, 5–5:15 p.m. (EST) with Mrs. Welthy Honsinger Fisher, as the speaker; Bernard Herrmann conducting the CBS concert orchestra.

Miss Maynor will deliver the prayer for the day. She will sing "Come Unto Him" and "How Beautiful Are the Feet of Them" from Handel's "The Messiah," and the traditional hymn sung on the occasion, "The Day Thou Gavest, Lord."

Seth McCoy
(1928–1997)

Seth McCoy was born on December 17, 1928, in Sanford, North Carolina, and died on January 22, 1997, of complications from a long illness. He was 68 years old. Prior to pursuing a career in vocal music he studied at the North Carolina Agricultural and Technical College. He then moved to the Cleveland Music School Settlement where he studied with Pauline Thesmacher. He then studied with Antonia Lavanne in New York. McCoy's reputation as one of America's premier oratorio soloists began during his tenure with the Robert Shaw Chorale (1963–1965) and the Bach Aria Group (1973–1980). In addition to serving as soloist with these ensembles, he appeared as soloist with many leading orchestras, including the New York Philharmonic, Boston Symphony Orchestra, Chicago Symphony Orchestra and Los Angeles Philharmonic. Zubin Mehta, Mstislav Rostropovich and Erich Leinsdorf are just a few of the conductors of note with whom he's worked. In 1978 he made his European debut at the Aldeburgh Festival. On February 17, 1979, he made his Metropolitan Opera debut in New York as Tamino in Mozart's *The Magic Flute.* Throughout his career he was honored with the Marian Anderson Scholarship, the Artist Advisory Council of Chicago Oratorio Award, the Martha Baird Rockefeller Grant and the Albert Schweitzer Medal for Artistry in Voice.

SOURCES

Currents: University of Rochester, University Public Relations (2-7-1997).
Smith, Eric Ledell: *Blacks in Opera: An Encyclopedia of People and Companies, 1873–1993* (Jefferson, N.C.: McFarland, 1994).

Robert McFerrin
(1921–)

Well, Robert and I came along together ... I was in St. Louis and he and I attended an *Elijah* that was prepared by Washington University, and we were sitting together for that. He's had a stroke and his memory is not as good, so a lot of times he'll have to have music, just for ordinary things to remind him, because his mind doesn't function quick enough from memory tragically. But the voice sounds glorious. He can still belt out *Eri tu* with all those high Gs. Just a glorious, glorious high baritone sound.

They said that when Bobby [Bobby McFerrin], the son of Robert McFerrin, started getting real famous someone asked Robert McFerrin, "Now what do you think of your son and those fabulous things that he's doing?"

"You know, he was doing that mess around the house all the time. I didn't think anything would come of it. I'm just as shocked as anybody else."

That's typical Robert McFerrin.

— William Warfield, April 21, 1994

Robert McFerrin, baritone, holds the distinct honor of being the first African American singer to land a permanent position with the Metropolitan Opera Company of New York. He debuted on January 27, 1955, in Verdi's *Aida* as Amonasro. Marian Anderson preceded him at the Metropolitan. However, she sang in one opera only. McFerrin was born on March 19, 1921, in Marianna, Arkansas. He studied at Fisk University in Nashville, Tennessee, from 1940 to 1941, at the Chicago Musical College where he received his Bachelor of Music degree in 1948, and at the Kathryn Turney Long School in New York in 1953. While in Chicago, he studied with George Graham. Catherine Van Burne was also one of his teachers. Winning first place in the *Chicago Tribune*'s national contest in 1942 gave McFerrin the opportunity to appear at the Chicagoland Music Festival. Throughout the 1940s and 1950s he appeared in numerous operas and Broadway musicals. He even performed with jazz orchestras. With Mary Cardwell Dawson's National Negro Opera Company, he sang the role of Amonasro in Verdi's *Aida* and Valentine in Gounod's *Faust*, in 1949 and 1952 respectively. He appeared with the New York City Opera Company in 1949 in a production of William Grant Still's *Troubled Island*. In 1950 he joined the New England Opera Company. His Broadway performances

Portrait of Robert McFerrin. Courtesy of the E. Azalia Hackley Collection, Detroit Public Library.

include noted composer Kurt Weill's *Lost in the Stars* in 1949, Marc Connelly's play *The Green Pastures* in 1951, and *My Darlin' Aida* in 1952. Hall Johnson composed the music for *The Green Pastures* production. For motion-picture director Otto Preminger's 1959 production of *Porgy and Bess,* McFerrin and Adele Addison, soprano, sang the title roles for the film soundtrack. He won the Metropolitan Auditions of the Air in 1953 and debuted with that company two years later. He has taught at the Sibelius Academy in Helsinki, Finland; Sacramento State College in California; the St. Louis Institute of Music Conservatory in Missouri; and Roosevelt University in Chicago. Robert McFerrin is the father of the popular recording artist Bobby McFerrin.

SOURCES

De Lerma, Dominique-René, *New Grove Dictionary of American Music* (New York: St. Martin's Press, 1986), Vol. 3, 147.
Southern, Eileen, *Biographical Dictionary of Afro-American and African Musicians* (Westport, CT: Greenwood Press, 1982), 258.

Musical America, February 1950, 282

Robert McFerrin opened this program with Monroe's *My Lovely Celia,* which he followed with Theseus's air, from Rameau's *Hippolyte et Arice.* In these he showed himself at once to be a singer of more than ordinary gifts. His voice was evenly matched throughout its range. His intonation was steady, and his control of breath and phrasing were excellent. A real

Portrait of Robert McFerrin. Courtesy of the E. Azalia Hackley Collection, Detroit Public Library.

dramatic sense manifested itself within the musical structure, heightening its intensity, yet never becoming the sort of ego-projection that results in distortion for the sake of histrionics. Schubert's Memnon and Fischerweise were excellently sung; and Florio and Der Zwerg were even more impressive in tonal control and interpretative finesse.

Mr. McFerrin's greatest liability appeared to be Jan Meyerowitz, his accompanist, whose insensitive rendering of the accompaniments would have wrecked all continuity and mood if the singer's line of control intensities had been less firm. Mr. Meyerowitz played havoc with tempos; but worse, he played a tentative pianissimo under the voice, and a clumsy banging fortissimo every time there was a piano interlude, regardless of the continuity or dynamic shape of the piece. Mr. McFerrin's gravest fault, of using only very loud or very soft singing, may well be a result of his rehearsal partner.

Two songs by Mr. Meyerowitz graced the program, To Egidius, and Declaration. The former was evasively sentimental, the second a kind of Broadway spiritual.

Abbie Mitchell
(1884–1960)

I never got to know Abbie Mitchell, but I'll share with you a story that Max Roach told me ... We were at the Jazz Educators convention in January, a year ago, and they had a big thing and he was giving anecdotes that Louis Armstrong had said. [With] Louis, you know, if it came up it came out. And so [Max Roach] said, "When I introduced [Louis Armstrong] to Abbie he looked at Abbie and said, 'Lady, if beauty was a disease, you'd be fucked up!'"

— *William Warfield, April 21, 1994*

Soprano Abbie Mitchell had one of the broadest and most diverse careers of all of the African American concert singers in the early twentieth century. Her musical career came to an end in 1935 when she sang the role of Clara in George Gershwin's opera *Porgy and Bess*. From that time on she taught and coached many singers in New York and appeared in many "spoken" dramatic roles on the stage.

Mitchell was born on September 25, 1884, in New York City. At the age of fourteen she joined Will Marion Cook's show *Clorindy or the Origin of the Cakewalk* in Chicago, Illinois, in 1898. This was the beginning of her professional career. Cook was her first husband and they were married from 1899 to 1906. She joined "Black Patti's Troubadours" in December of 1898 and had leading roles in many top shows of the era throughout the turn of the century. To name a few: *Jes Lak White Folks* (1899) by Cook, *In Dahomey* (1902) by George Walker and Bert Williams, and *The*

Portrait of Abbie Mitchell. Photographs and Prints Division, Schomburg Center for Research in Black Culture, The New York Public Library, Astor, Lenox and Tilden Foundations.

Red Moon by Bob Cole and Rosamund and James Weldon Johnson. For *In Dahomey* she went to London, England. In 1905 and 1908 she toured Europe as a member of the original and second edition Memphis Students ensemble.

Harry T. Burleigh, the noted African American concert baritone, pianist, and composer, was Mitchell's first major voice teacher in New York. She later studied with Emilia Serrano and with the world renowned Jean de Reszke in Paris. She also coached with Cook, her husband, and Melville Charlton.

Eventually the spoken theater would gain some of her attention and talent. Around 1910 she began appearing in plays at the Pekin and Monogram Theaters in Chicago. In 1914 she became a charter member of the original Lafayette Players of Harlem, New York. In addition to these endeavors she maintained a busy singing career, appearing frequently in New York and Washington, D.C. For a brief moment in her career her singing came to a halt due to many years of vocal strain in Vaudeville and musical comedy. When she returned to opera and the concert stage she appeared as Marguerite in Charles Gounod's *Faust*.

From 1919 to 1921 she toured the United States and abroad with Cook's Southern Syncopated Orchestra (or the New York Syncopated Orchestra). When the tour concluded she remained in Europe and toured for over a year with her own act, "Abbie Mitchell and Her Full Harmonic Quartet." At that time she studied voice in Paris once again and later returned in 1931 for additional vocal training. Her opera and concert singing career was interrupted briefly when she taught voice at the famous Tuskegee Institute in Alabama from 1932 to 1934. In 1934 she appeared with the Aeolian Opera, singing the role of Santuzza in a production of Mascagni's *Cavalleria Rusticana*. The following year she gave her farewell "musical-stage" performance as Clara in the 1935 production of George Gershwin's *Porgy and Bess*.

SOURCES

Cuney-Hare, Maud, *Negro Musicians and Their Music* (Washington, D.C.: Da Capo Press, 1936), 369–371.

Southern, Eileen, *Biographical Dictionary of Afro-American and African Musicians* (Westport, CT: Greenwood Press, 1982), 275–276.

"Abbie Mitchell Fine in New B'way Play," *New York Amsterdam News*, 4 March 1939, 17

A poignant, revealing picture of the decadent South at the turn of the twentieth century is painted with bold, sure strokes in "The Little Foxes," a drama in three acts by Lillian Hellman, featuring two talented Negro actors, Abbie Mitchell and John Marlott, and starring glamorous Tallulah Bankhead at the National Theatre.

Harlemites may well recoil at the frequent use of the word "nigger" throughout the play. That is only natural.

But when the characters of those who use the despicable word are properly and intelligently interpreted only a deep disgust and hatred for southern "aristocracy" can possibly result.

Depicting with uncanny and crystalline clarity the characters of members of the crude Southern family which attempts to barge its way to millions by exploiting Negro labor and lying and cheating each other, the play sweeps on to a thrilling, breathless climax which includes all the elements of melodrama and presages complete ruin for the Hubbard family.

To Miss Hellman, a brilliant and forthright playwright who disrobes without sympathy or compassion the mean souls of her leading characters, the Hubbard family is undoubtedly the symbol of a South that must crumble on its own flimsy foundation.

The attitude of the white Southerner toward the Negro and the Negro's own intelligent interpretation of that attitude, is expressed in one short sentence read with great feeling and depth by Miss Mitchell.

She says, in answer to her employer's statement that he was sorry that he was unable to leave her a large sum of money in his will: "Dat's all right, Mr. Horace, white folks would take it away from me anyway."

Only four characters in the whole play stand out clean and untarnished. They are Addie, played by Miss Mitchell; Birdie Hubbard, played by Patricia Collings; Alexandra Giddens, played by Florence Williams; and Horace Giddens, played by Frank Conroy.

Miss Bankhead, herself a Southerner and daughter of the present Speaker of the House of Representatives in Washington, plays one of the most unsympathetic roles in her brilliant and admirable career. She manages to make you hate her Regina Giddens with a tempestuous hate — which, by the way, is one of the greatest compliments which may be paid a great actress.

Without the sympathetic and intelligent interpretations of the servants, Addie and Cal, played by Miss Mitchell and Mr. Marriott, "The Little Foxes" could not be complete. Although Miss Mitchell's role is by far the larger and most difficult, the homely humor of Cal serves to make the audience stand the melodramatic pace of the play.

Other members of the Hubbard family, Oscar, Leo and Benjamin, are played with compelling audacity by Carl Benton Reid, Dan Duryea and Charles Dingle. The play is staged by Herman Shumlin, settings designed by Howard Bay and costumes by Aline Bernstein.

Every Harlemite would travel down to Forty-first street to see "The Little Foxes" and hail the author for pulling the frail clothing from Mr. and Mrs. Southern Aristocracy and showing them for what they are — mean, little people who certainly must shrivel up and die.

"Abbie Mitchell to Be Honored at Party," *New York Amsterdam News*, 7 October 1939, 16

Miss Abbie Mitchell, playing one of the lead parts in Tallulah Bankhead's "The Little Foxes," will be given a party at the Sky Club this Thursday night, honoring her for her long and continued work on the Stage and for her more than a year's run on Broadway.

Mrs. Florence K. Williamson-Norman of the National Council of Negro Women and Lambda Kappa Mu sorority; Mrs. Bessy Mearden and John H. Thompson of the Associated Negro Press are to be hosts.

Included in the party will be Tallulah Bankhead, Olsen and Johnson of "Hellzapoppin,'" Donald Heywood and Ethel Harris of "Carribean Cruise," Dr. and Mrs. Lynwood Henry and Dr. and Mrs. Roan.

A special floorshow has been readied.

"Abbie Mitchell Tells of First Negro Singer at Carnegie Hall, Recalling Famed *Black Patti*," *New York Amsterdam News*, 8 June 1940, 16

"The place — Carnegie Hall, the singer — Sissieretta Jones, the time — well, long before you and I were born," Abbie Mitchell was living again the story she heard as the girl wife of Will Marion Cook.

"Yes," she continued, "Mr. Cook was a very young man at the time. He had just returned from Europe as a brilliant violinist. He played on the program on this memorable night in New York's Carnegie Hall. The house was packed to hear the first Negro woman singer who had ever appeared on the stage of that hall. Her name was Sissieretta Jones. When she had finished her performance, the elder Cornelius Vanderbilt rose from his seat and cried out: "I dub you 'Black Patti' (Adelina Patti was the reigning singer of the day), and presented her with a check for $5.00 for further voice cultivation.

In answer to the question as to whether Black Patti was the first Negro prima donna, Miss Mitchell mentioned Madame Selika, but reminded us that Madame Selika went to Europe and became European, actually leaving the field to Sissieretta Jones who came somewhat later.

"In like manner do we think of the Negro theatre," said the plump little singer-actress, with eyes sparkling and shapely hands moving expressively, warming to her subject. "One thinks first of the Pekin theatre group or the Pekin stock company as the first Negro theatre for the drama.

The Shakespearean theatre group antedated them by many years, of course, but that was too long ago," she laughingly observed.

Abbie Mitchell is remembered as the petite soubrette or ingenue with the beautiful voice who sang "Red, Red Rose" and made many of the famous Will Marion Cook numbers the hits that they were.

The Pekin theatre stock company of Chicago turned the tide for Negroes in the drama. Before the advent of this group of players, white actors made up dark for Negro parts in dramatic plays. The tide was turned by the Pekin stock company, but it was not fully so until about four years after when the Lafayette players were formed. Both of these organizations were responsible for the place that the Negro holds in the field of drama today.

Won't Return to N.Y. Miss Mitchell will not return to New York with the cast of "The Little Foxes," which stars Tallulah Bankhead, when the show closes here on Saturday after a seven week run, but will remain here to act as technical adviser and to play the part of Abbie Mitchell in the American Negro Exposition's production, "Cavalcade of the Negro Theatre," being written by Langston Hughes and Arna Bontomps.

The theatre exhibit is only one of hundreds, which will be on view for the people of America at the Coliseum in Chicago from July 4 to Labor Day, September 2.

"Abbie Mitchell Goes to Perpetual *Summertime*," *New York Amsterdam News*, 26 March 1960, 4

They sang the songs Abbie Mitchell made famous during her career in the theatre and on the concert stage at memorial service held Sunday afternoon.

Helen Dowdy of the Negro Actors Guild sang "Summertime," the song Miss Mitchell sang in the original cast of "Porgy and Bess."

Walter Richardson, one of her former voice students, sang "Mammy," a song written by her late husband, Will Marion Cook, with lyrics by Lester Walton, former minister to Liberia and a song hit the early part of the century.

Lucille Birnie sang "Rose in the Bud" and "Sometimes I Feel Like a Motherless Child," two songs Miss Mitchell sang when she was among the first Negro artists to be heard on a coast to coast network.

Pianist Play. Beatrice Rippy sang other tunes Miss Mitchell was famous for introducing. Lucky Roberts played several on the piano; so did Eubie Blake, Marc D'Albert, Carrol Hollister and Dr. Douglass Speaks. Leigh Whipper reviewed her life in the theatre. The funeral home was overcrowded.

Miss Mitchell, one of the pioneer Negro artists of the theatre and concert stage, died last Wednesday night at Harlem Hospital after a long illness. She was 76 and had been in poor health for two years.

A Solemn Requiem Mass was sung for her Monday morning at St. Joseph's Roman Catholic Church and she was buried in St. Raymond's Cemetery in the Bronx. Her casket was covered with a blanket of orchids; the church was also filled. Actress Tallulah Bankhead sent a floral piece and a tribute.

Pallbearers included Dr. Robert Weaver, John A. Davis Leigh, Whipper, Dr. Donald Milberb, Leland Marshall and Theodore Harris.

Before Royalty. During her career, Miss Mitchell had the distinction of appearing in three command performances before the royalty of Europe, twice in London and once in St. Petersburg, Russia. At the first she was only 17 years old.

A native of Baltimore, Md., she was raised in a convent in that city. At 14 she landed a part in Paul Lawrence Dunbar's "Chlorindy" which had music written by Will Marion Cook whom she later married. This show was billed as "The Origin of the Cakewalk."

Miss Mitchell was known as the "Little Girl with the Big Voice."

In 1912, Miss Mitchell became one of the original members of the Lafayette Players and played for several years in its repertory group. After spending a few years devoted exclusively to appearances on the concert stage, she taught voice at Tuskegee Institute and at Atlanta University.

Returns to Theatre. She returned to the theatre in the 1930s and appeared in "Abraham's Bosom," "Coquette," and "Mulatto," "On Whiteman Avenue," "Porgy and Bess," among other plays.

In recent years she had taught voice and coached singers at a West 125th St. studio until about five years ago when her eyesight began to fail.

She is survived by a son, Dr. Mercer Cook, Sr., professor of Romance Languages at Howard University, now on leave doing research on African Leadership in Paris, France; and three grandchildren: Mrs. Marion Douglas Quick, a teacher in the NYC public school system; Mercer Cook, Jr., an attorney of Chicago; and Jacques Cook, a student in Paris, France.

Nellie Brown Mitchell
(1845 — 1924)

Soprano Nellie Brown was born in Dover, New Hampshire, in 1845. While in Dover she studied with Caroline Bracket, who encouraged her to pursue a professional vocal career. Her career as a singer began at the

Free-Will Baptist Church, an Anglo-American church in Dover, in 1865. Brown was the soprano soloist. Service to the church would prove to be a distinct part of her musical career. In 1872 she left Free-Will Baptist to serve as soloist for Grace Church in Haverhill, Massachusetts. She remained there until 1876, returned to Dover, and then served as musical director from 1879 to c1886 at the Bloomfield Street Church in Boston, Massachusetts. While in Massachusetts, around 1874, Brown studied voice with Mrs. J. Rametti and Professor O'Neill. In Boston she studied at the New England Conservatory and the School of Vocal Arts. She received her diploma in 1879. In 1874 she gave a series of successful recitals in Boston and made her New York debut at Steinway Hall. In 1882 she debuted in Philadelphia, Pennsylvania. From 1882 to 1885 Brown was "prima-donna soprano" with James Bergen's Star Concerts. Flora Batson replaced her when Mitchell had prior concert obligations in the South and could not attend a performance in Providence, Rhode Island. She resigned her church position in 1886 and devoted her time to her concert career and her newly formed Nellie Brown Mitchell Concert Company. Her husband, Lieutenant Charles L. Mitchell, was part of the Fifty-fifth Massachusetts Negro regiment. Soprano Ednah B. Brown, her sister, was a member of her concert company.

During the 1880s and into the 1890s Brown reached the peak of her concert career. Her reputation and fame won her great admiration from colleagues and critics. She was considered by many to be the greatest African American singer and Madame Marie Selika's only rival. She concertized often throughout the East Coast and the Middle West. For many summers she taught at the Hedding Chautauqua Summer School in East Epping, New Hampshire. In the 1890s she retired from the concert stage and devoted her time to private teaching, advertising the "Guilmette Method" of vocal technique. She died in Boston in January of 1924.

SOURCES

Cuney-Hare, Maud, *Negro Musicians and Their Music* (Washington, D.C.: Da Capo Press, 1936).
De Lerma, Dominique-René, *The New Grove Dictionary of American Music* (New York: St. Martin's Press, 1986), Vol. 1, 310.
Southern, Eileen, *Biographical Dictionary of Afro-American and African Musicians* (Westport, CT: Greenwood Press, 1982), 275–276.

Margaret Montgomery

"Margaret Montgomery, Contralto, April 5,"
Musical America, 5 April 1947, 10

Margaret Montgomery, contralto, a Negro of obviously fine gifts, made her New York debut in the Town Hall with Paul Ulanowsky at the piano. Miss Montgomery, in spite of considerable study does not invariably place her voice at its best advantage, nor did it seem wholly wise to open with the soprano aria from Gluck's Alceste. But the following, "Es Ist Vollbracht" from the St. John Passion was done well and with good tone, as was the Furibondo aria from Handel's Partenope. The second group was by Schubert, Brahms and Strauss. Of these the Minnelied of Brahms was especially good. The next group was by Rachmaninoff, Gliere and Villa-Lobos and the final one by Price and Kerr. Much of Miss Montgomery's singing was of a high order as she has evidently had excellent coaching and possesses natural musicianship. Her reception was most cordial.

Charlotte Wallace Murray

Charlotte Wallace Murray was born in Columbia, South Carolina. From 1906 to 1915 she taught in Washington, D.C. and was a church singer. While in Washington, she studied voice, piano, and harmony, subsequently giving concerts throughout the area. Some years after her marriage to Dr. Peter Murray, in 1915, the couple moved to New York City. She continued her musical studies there and gave local concerts. In 1926 she sang the role of the "Queen" in Frank Harling's opera, *Deep River.* This was the first opera to be given with a mixed cast in the United States. Baritone Jules Bledsoe played opposite Murray as the King. For her portrayal of Katinka in Gilbert and Sullivan's *Mikado* the Institute of Musical Art awarded her the Faculty Scholarship. In 1931 she graduated from the institute after having won a second scholarship.

SOURCES

Cuney-Hare, Maud, *Negro Musicians and Their Music* (Washington, D.C.: Da Capo Press, 1936), 378–379.

"Noted Contralto Heard at Fisk — Charlotte Wallace Murray Gets Critic's Praise," *New York Amsterdam News,* 11 March 1939, 16

> The Nashville Tennesseean had the following to say of Charlotte Wallace Murray's recital at Fisk. "Her voice has a beautiful quality with ringing high notes of great power and magnificent chest tones. Her singing of Brahms and Strauss lieder stamped her as an artist with splendid interpretive ability. These songs were done with such splendor of tone and depth of feeling that they brought rounds of applause. After a group of spirituals she gave three encores including two played to her own accompaniment."

Camille Nickerson
(1887–1982)

> The branch of the National Association of Negro Musicians [NANM] that they say is actually a year older than the NANM itself was formed by Camille Nickerson. And then, of course, later on she has been president of the NANM. Her big thing was writing, especially Creole songs. Marvelous things she's written.
>
> *— William Warfield, April 21, 1994*

Camille Nickerson was born in New Orleans, Louisiana, on March 30, 1887. She received her formal musical training from Oberlin College in Ohio. At Oberlin she received a Bachelor of Arts and a Master of Arts degree. From 1916 to 1926 she taught at her father's school, the Nickerson School of Music. "My father told me after I finished Oberlin, 'Now you come back home and teach. Everybody can't go to Oberlin, so you bring Oberlin down to us.'"

From 1926 to 1962 she taught at Howard University in Washington, D.C. During the 1930s Nickerson began collecting Creole folksongs. "Professor Nickerson, herself of Creole extraction, has devoted much effort to the collection and preservation of Creole folk music. She wrote her master's thesis at Oberlin College on the subject and since that time has made many arrangements of the songs."

With the help of a Rosenwald Foundation grant, Nickerson was able to tour the United States and abroad, giving concerts of the pieces she collected. She called herself "The Louisiana Lady" and accompanied herself at the piano. Some of her arrangements have been published. Throughout her career she also accompanied other African American artists of note, including E. Azalia Hackley, Anita Patti Brown, Joseph Douglass, and Clarence Cameron White.

Many singers of note have also sung her songs:

> Having collected the songs, I was anxious to have them sung. I searched for singers. I remember Mr. [Roland] Hayes was so delighted when Dr. [Alain] Locke took me to visit him when he was here one time for a concert. I sang many of the songs, and he seemed very pleased, and later on he made a record of the *Banjo Song*. Songs have been sung by the Fisk Jubilee Singers, Margaret Tynes, Lawrence Winters, Mattiwilda Dobbs, Camilla Williams, Roland Hayes, Todd Duncan, and Mme. [Lillian] Evanti.

Camille Nickerson gave her first major concert in Times Hall in New York in 1944. She also sang in Kimball Hall in Chicago, Kiel Hall in St. Louis, the Phillips Gallery in Washington, D.C., and at numerous colleges and universities. She also toured France. From 1935 to 1937 she was president of the National Association of Negro Musicians. She died on April 27, 1982, in Washington, D.C.

SOURCES

Black Perspective in Music, Vol. 7, No. 1, pp. 82 and 87.
McGinty, Doris, *"Conversation with ... Camille Nickerson, the Louisiana Lady,"* *The Black Perspective in Music*, Vol. 7, No. 1, 81
Obituary: *The Black Perspective in Music*, Vol. 10, No. 2, 230.

Aubrey Pankey

Baritone Aubrey Pankey was born in Pittsburgh, Pennsylvania, where he first studied voice and sang in an Episcopalian church choir as a boy soprano. His formal training took place at the historic Hampton Institute in Virginia. While there he was influenced and encouraged to pursue musical heights by the noted African American musician Dr. R. Nathaniel Dett. Pankey went on to continue his studies at the Oberlin Conservatory of Music in Ohio and at Boston University in Massachusetts. He studied voice with Arthur Hubbard in Boston and with John Alan Haughton in New York. On January 26, 1930, he gave a recital at Jordan Hall, which evoked the needed momentum to study abroad. From 1931 to 1940 he lived in Europe, performing as well as studying. He studied with Theodore Lierhammer in Vienna, Austria, and with Oscar Daniel and Charles Panzera in Paris, France.

"Josef Reitler wrote of him in the *Neue Freie Presse* of November 23, 1931, 'He is the possessor of a musical soul, which in glowing manner is able to approach Schubert and Richard Strauss with a feeling and understanding worthy of a born German. Colorful expression is skillfully combined with a natural mellowness of voice.'

"Robert Konta in the Weiner *Allgemeine Zeitung* of November 26, 1931, designated him 'A black man who sings Schubert and Richard Strauss with overwhelming intensity of feeling and forms them into great unforgettable experiences. He is a boon for our period where one is very easily inclined to see in all Negro musicians mere Jazzband Clowns. There are evidently black men who are messengers of culture at its greatest'" (Cuney-Hare, 383).

Pankey made his debut at New York's Town Hall in 1940. Tours throughout the United States and Europe followed. The United States Office of the Coordinator of Inter-American Affairs sponsored a tour for him throughout South America. The Chinese People's Association for Cultural Relations with foreign countries invited him to tour China in 1956. As a result, he was the first American to do so since the establishment of the Republic of China in 1949.

Aubrey Pankey died in New York City.

SOURCES

Cuney-Hare, Maud, *Negro Musicians and Their Music* (Washington, D.C.: Da Capo Press, 1936), 382–383.
Southern, Eileen, *Biographical Dictionary of Afro-American and African Musicians* (Westport, CT: Greenwood Press, 1982), 299.

"Nine Years in Europe Alters Singer's View," *New York Amsterdam News,* 17 February 1939, 5

The Statue of Liberty looked pretty good to Aubrey Pankey, celebrated young negro baritone, when he returned to New York a month or so ago after a highly successful and exciting nine year sojourn abroad.

The majestic symbol of American peace and democracy looked good to him even though it was in Europe and not in America that he finally tasted success where he sang his way into the hearts of music lovers in almost all of the major metropolitan centers of the Old World.

You see, Mr. Pankey has experienced many things which have won his young naivete from his breast since he left this country in 1930 for a European tour which was to last only a year and a half. And so he returns to these shores sobered and with a new perspective on life.

The Other Half. In the troublesome years since he has been away, years of great human suffering and economic depression, which have seen the beginning of another world conflict for power — he has been able to observe how the other half of the world lives and has been able to rationalize problems which may have puzzled him.

Portrait of Aubrey Pankey. Courtesy of the E. Azalia Hackley Collection, Detroit Public Library.

Let him tell you about a few of these things in his own words. "I find that the Negro isn't the only minority group having difficulties," he remarked this week.

"Most Negroes," he went on, "are so enmeshed in their own problems that it is only when they get away that they are able to gain perspective and learn that if social and economic discrimination is not directed toward them, it is directed toward someone else.

"In Europe I saw things happen to Jews that Negroes have never experienced in this country. Atrocities toward Negroes usually occur in small, benighted communities of the South, but the Jew undergoes the grossest of indignities in such cosmopolitan centers as Berlin, Dresden, and Munich.

"For instance, in Vienna, I saw a Jewish student thrown out of a seven story window and in the same city I saw Jewish women who dared to attend the opera forced to scrub streets in their evening clothes. In Linz,

I saw a young cultured Gentile woman, the wife of a Jew, walking the streets wearing a placard on her back reading 'I am the mistress of a Jew.'"

The young singer, himself, had quite an experience in Salzburg, Austria, in 1932, right at the beginning of the Nazi regime. On the morning of his scheduled concert there were demonstrations in the streets of the town against his recital at Mozart Concert Hall. "Fifty policemen escorted me to the concert and back to my hotel," he recounted, "and people who wished to attend the concert were given police protection. I was given police protection until I left town the next day."

Mr. Pankey, whose European headquarters during the past six years have been in France, where he also gained quite a reputation as a motion picture actor, hasn't been in Germany since 1934.

Likes German People. "Germans on the whole," he said, "are fine people and I like them and their customs tremendously. Unfortunately they are the puppets of a degenerate regime. As a matter of fact, in Germany, it is the younger people, blindly enthusiastic about a great cause who perpetrate the atrocities about which you read in the papers."

The young baritone was barred from Italy despite the fact that a tour had been arranged, after the attack on Graziani in 1937. He has the distinction of being the first American Negro to sing in Jerusalem where the *Palestine Post* critic said of him:

"His voice is dark and warm, full of the forte effects and almost mysterious in the fine pianos and pianissimos."

Speaking of his visit to Palestine, the singer remarked that he "seemed to be following trouble." He arrived in that country at the height of the trouble between the Arabs and the Jews. He said that he used to wear a fox when he went into the Arab quarters of the towns and that he was often mistaken for a native.

Mistaken for Arab. "One day I was roaming around a little town near Rehovath," he said. "There had been trouble there earlier in the day when the Arabs came out of the hills and raided some of the outlying houses. All of a sudden I found myself in the center of a crowd who began looking at me curiously. They took me for an Arab who had no business in that section of the city. I was wondering what I should do when someone in the crowd remarked: 'Oh that's the colored singer who came to sing for us.' Then they quietly dispersed."

The trouble between the Arabs and the Jews, Mr. Pankey commented, was instigated by Italy and Germany to keep unrest in Palestine.

"There is no conceivable reason that Arabs and Jews should not get along together," he remarked. "They lived together previously for hundreds of years in peace. It is simply a political maneuver of the fascist countries who pay the Arab chieftains to make disturbance."

The baritone said that he found some sort of prejudice in evidence in every country, if not against race, then against class. France, he said was the most free country he visited as far as race is concerned, but there are class distinctions to be found there.

"The people of France and all of the central European counties don't want war," Mr. Pankey declared.

Want No Peace. "The governments are confiscating any organ advocating peace. The first air raid over Paris was a fiasco," he commented. "As a matter of fact, they had to come right back the next day to frighten the people. Airplanes are being used mostly to spread propaganda and not bombs."

Mr. Pankey began his singing career when he was very young as a boy soprano in a church choir in Pittsburgh. When his parents died, he went to Hampton Institute to become a mechanical engineer. It was there that his voice was discovered and after warm encouragement from many musicians, including Roland Hayes, he began to study music seriously.

He then attended Oberlin Conservatory, the Hubbard Studios in Boston and the Boston University College of Music. In Europe, he studied in Vienna and in Paris where he was a student of Professor Oscar Daniel.

He hopes to arrange a concert tour here this spring.

"I am glad to be home from several points of view. Even if the war hadn't broken out. I had planned to come back anyway, I feel that it is time to do some things in America since it is the world's greatest music center."

"Air Lane Guest," *New York Amsterdam News,* 4 October 1941, 22

Aubrey Pankey, internationally famous baritone, who will be heard over WNYC this Sunday, October 5, at 1:30 p.m. when he sings with the New York City Symphony under the direction of Zoltan Fekete. During the hour and a half program, Mr. Pankey will sing Gounod's "Aria from Faust" Tschaikovsky's "Don Juan Serenade" and "Follow Me," a derivative by Dett. The program, free to the public, will emanate from the Brooklyn Museum. The singer will also appear the following Wednesday afternoon at 2:30 with the same orchestra at Museum of Natural History on Central Park West. This program, also free to the public, will not be broadcast.

"Pankey to Sing at Dvorak Fete," *New York Amsterdam News,* 8 November 1941, 18

Aubrey Pankey, baritone, will be the featured soloist at the Anton Dvorak Centennial Celebration to be held at the Studios of Music Education, 9 West 82 Street Friday night. Paul Stefan, dean of Viennese music critics and biographer of Dvorak, Mahler and Toscanini, will speak; Wilson Vance, translator of Dvorak's "Life" into English, will act as master of ceremonies.

Mr. Pankey will sing American music, which tended to influence Dvorak during his stay in this country. It was through Harry Burleigh that Dvorak was made aware of the best beauty of the Negro Spiritual, to extent of perpetuating it in his "New World Symphony" and other of his compositions.

Besides Mr. Pankey's contribution of two Dvorak songs and four Negro Spirituals to the program, Yella Braun-Fernwald, contralto, will sing his Biblical songs, and Hinda Barnett, violinist, and Anton Rovinsky, pianist, will play "Sonatina — Opus 100"; Judith Sander, soprano, will sing Moravian folk songs.

"Otto Herz, accompanist, Carnegie Hall, Jan. 31, evening," *Musical America,* 10 February 1944, 210

Mr. Pankey gave, in effect, two recitals, of which the second was immeasurably better. It took him some time to gain his poise and get his voice under effective control. Unquestionably he would have been vastly more at ease in a smaller house. As it was, the yawning spaces of Carnegie Hall tempted him through much of the first half of the concert to strain his upper tones, to their inevitable detriment. Nor did he find it easy to adjust the intimate, confiding nature of his singing and the subtler aspects of his interpretative manner to the unsympathetic dimensions of an auditorium which so often futilizes the very qualities in which a singer like Mr. Pankey excels. Hence the softer tones of his lower and medium range were frequently almost inaudible, well planned nuances failed to achieve their purpose and repeatedly the upper part of his scale appeared forced.

Nevertheless, in spite of handicaps, Mr. Pankey managed to convey in certain of his German Lieder a clear impression that he understood their style and sensed their moods.

His intonation, incidentally, was secure even as it had been during the earlier and less convincing part of the recital. The closing group of Spirituals, one of the best features of the evening, profited as such things always do, by a more naive and elemental than "arty" approach.

The audience acclaimed Mr. Pankey with increasing warmth and he was induced to contribute several encores, among them a marching song popular among the Soviet troops and the tragic "Lied de Moor Soldaten" of the German concentration camp victims, which he sang partly in English translation and ended in the German original.

In Otto Herz he had a fine-feeling and sympathetic accompanist.

Musical America, 10 January 1945, 14

Aubrey Pankey, baritone, opened the series of recitals in the auditorium of Hunter College on the evening of Dec. 9, with Otto Herz at the piano. Mr. Pankey began with a group of classical works, all in Italian except "Love in Thy Youth" by Howard. The best sung of the group was Caccini's "Amarilli, mia Bella." Of the second group, Schubert's "Wohin" was excellent and the Strauss "Standchen" was a really fine piece of singing in every respect. Songs by Chausson and Duparc were well received and Debussy's "noel des Enfants qui n'mont plus de Maisons," which Mr. Pankey read out in English, was appropriate and was well sung. For an aria, Mr. Pankey offered the overfamiliar "Vision Fugitive" from "Herodiade" and the list ended with the customary Spirituals, one of which, "Wade in de Water," was arranged by the singer. It was an evening of sensitive and musicianly singing, throughout.

Louise Parker
(1925–1986)

In 1950, Louise Parker, contralto, became the first African American to graduate from the Curtis Institute of Music. She received a Bachelor of Music degree.

She was born in Philadelphia in 1925, and throughout her early years studied music, sang in church choirs, and even won a Marian Anderson Music Scholarship. As a soloist with the Hall Johnson Choir she had her first taste of the professional level of her career. The choir toured extensively throughout the United States and abroad. Parker continued her studies in Europe and performed widely as a concert singer. Her New York debut came in 1958. She has performed with many American and European opera companies and has appeared as soloist with the world's major symphony orchestras.

SOURCES

Obituary: *The Black Perspective in Music,* Vol. 14, No. 3, 326.

Willis Patterson
(1930–)

Willis Patterson, bass-baritone, joined the faculty at the University of Michigan in 1968. During his tenure there he served as professor of voice, chairman of the voice department, and associate dean of music. Prior to that position he taught at Southern University in Louisana and Virginia State College. He has concertized with many orchestras and performed with numerous opera companies throughout Europe and the United States. He was a Fulbright Fellow and a winner of the Marian Anderson Award for young singers. Mr. Patterson appeared as King Balthazar in the NBC-TV production of *Amahl and the Night Visitors* by Gian Carlo Menotti. His opera credits include Porgy in *Porgy and Bess* by Gershwin, Rocco in *Fidelio* by Beethoven, and Colline in Puccini's *La Bohème*. He has served as vice-president and president of the National Association of Negro Musicians, and as executive secretary of the National Black Music Caucus.

Desseria Broadley Plato
(d. 1907)

The details concerning Desseria Plato's career are not known. However, when she attracted attention she did so on a grand scale. During the last decade of the nineteenth century Plato was making a name for herself as a concert singer. In Signor A. Farini's Grand Creole and Colored Opera and Concert Company she was billed as a "prima donna mezzo-soprano." With Farini's company she sang the role of Azucena in Verdi's *Il Trovatore* at the Union Square Theatre in New York. As a substitute for Sissieretta Jones, at a concert given on Colored American Day (August 25, 1893) at the Chicago World's Fair, she again gained much attention. In 1896 Plato joined John Isham's Oriental American Company. Sidney Woodward and Mattie Wilkes (died 1927 in New York) were also members of this opera troupe.

SOURCES

Southern, Eileen, *Biographical Dictionary of Afro-American and African Musicians* (Westport, CT: Greenwood Press, 1982), 309.

Leontyne Price
(1927–)

Leontyne Price has been hailed by many as the greatest American soprano of the second half of the twentieth century. Indeed, she commanded the respect and admiration of audiences and critics around the world, equaling such contemporaries as Renata Tebaldi, Joan Sutherland and Maria Callas. No other African American singer has to date achieved the level of Price's international celebrity.

Mary Violet Leontyne Price was born on February 10, 1927, in Laurel, Mississippi. At an early age she was taught piano by a local woman and also learned to sing. After graduating from Oak Park High School in 1944 she enrolled in the College of Education and Industrial Arts in Wilberforce, Ohio. There she studied voice with Catherine Van Buren and received her Bachelor of Arts degree in 1948. A scholarship enabled her to study at the Juilliard School of Music in New York. She studied with Florence Page Kimball and performed in the Opera Workshop under the direction of Frederic Cohen. Her performance as Mistress Ford in Verdi's *Falstaff* brought her to the attention of Virgil Thomson. Thomson subsequently invited her to sing in the revival of his opera *4 Saints in 3 Acts* on Broadway in 1952. Her Mistress Ford performance also came to the attention of baritone William Warfield and the producers of a soon-to-be revival of *Porgy and Bess.* Warfield and the producers agreed to engage Price as Bess. The revival commenced at the Ziegfeld Theatre in 1953, and a two-year tour followed. On November 14, 1954, she made her debut as a concert singer, singing in the first performance of Samuel Barber's *Prayers of Kierkegaard* with the Boston symphony Orchestra under the direction of Charles Munch. She achieved national acclaim on January 23, 1955. when she performed the title role in *Tosca* on the NBC television network. A successful career was a forgone conclusion as a result. She made her debut with the San Francisco Opera in 1957 as Madame Lidoine in the American premiere of *Dialogues des Carmelites.* Aida, Leonora (Il Trovatore), Orff's Die Kluge, and Donna Elvira followed this role with the company. She sang Aida with the Vienna State Opera under the direction of Herbert von Karajan; on July 2, 1958, she sang Aida once again at Covent Garden in London and performed the role again at La Scala in Milan in 1959. Her La Scala debut made her the first African American woman to sing with the historic company. She also debuted in Verona, Salzburg and Chicago during this period. On January 27, 1961, Leontyne Price made her Metropolitan Opera debut in the role of Leonora (*Il Trovatore*). Her performance received a 42-minute ovation, the longest in the Opera Company's history. Aida, Tosca, Donna Anna, Pamina and Madama Butterfly were soon to follow. She sang the role of Cleopatra in the premiere of Samuel Barber's *Antony and Cleopatra* at the opening of the new Metropolitan Opera House at Lincoln Center on September 16, 1966. She added the title role in *Manon Lescaut* to her repertoire at the Met on February 7, 1975. On January 3, 1985, she sang Aida in her farewell performance in opera in a televised live broadcast from the Metropolitan Opera. Price was married to baritone William Warfield in 1952. They separated in 1959 and were divorced in 1973. Throughout her prestigious career, Leontyne Price received numerous awards and honors, including the Presidential Medal of Freedom, the National Medal of Arts, the Kennedy Center Lifetime Achievement Award and 18 Grammy Awards — a record among opera singers.

SOURCES

Blyth, A., "Leontyne Price Talks," *Gramophone, xlix* (1971), 303.
Lyon, H., *L.P.: Highlights of a Prima Donna* (New York, 1973).
Steane, J.B., *The Grand Tradition* (London, 1974), 407ff.
Steins, R., *L.P. Opera Superstar* (Woodbridge, Connecticut, 1993).

Muriel Rahn
(1911–1961)

I met her through *Carmen Jones.* She was in the Broadway production. Muriel Smith and Muriel Rahn [were double cast in the production]. Muriel Rahn I think was the first one that did it. And the reason I met both of them, I was in the service, in military intelligence, and Billy Rose was getting ready to put on this production of *Carmen Jones.* And he actually personally called the post that I was on, [I knew] because later on word got around that Billy Rose had called this private Warfield ... I went in [to New York] and auditioned for him. They wanted me to do Husky Miller. And Billy Rose tried to have me assigned to special services and then let them put me on leave to do the Broadway show. And they said, "Oh, Mr. Rose, we never could do that, turn a soldier over to you to use in a Broadway production." I didn't think it would work, but it's interesting, because from that audition John Hammand, who was a great producer and entrepreneur, heard me. And years later, after I got out of the service, he was the one who was instrumental in getting the people from *Call Me Mister* to call me. [They] found out where I was, at Eastman studying for my masters, and brought me down to New York to audition ... I met John Hammond at that time and it was at that time that I met Muriel Rahn and Muriel Smith. And they were both excellent.

— *William Warfield, April 21, 1994*

Muriel Rahn, soprano, was born in Boston, Massachusetts, in 1911 and moved to New York, as a child, with her family. There she received her formal education. Her musical education was a product of her studies at Tuskegee Institute in Alabama, Atlanta University in Georgia, and the Music Conservatory of the University of Nebraska at Lincoln.

Her professional career began with the Eva Jessye Dixie Jubilee Singers in 1929. Various Broadway musicals soon followed. Numbered among them were Lew Leslie's *Blackbirds of 1929,* Connie Inn's *Hot Chocolates* in 1929, and *Carmen Jones* in 1943. Rahn and soprano Muriel Smith sang the title role in alternation in the original 1943 Broadway production. Opera entered her professional career in the 1940s when she became a member of the opera group of the National Orchestral Association in New York. Some of the organization's productions in which Rahn appeared were *The Abduction from the Seraglio* by Mozart, and *Suor Angelica* and *Gianni Schichi* by Puccini. The title role in Verdi's *Aida* came to her in 1948 with the Salmaggi Opera. This experience was repeated with the San Carlo Opera in 1949, and with Mary Cardwell Dawson's renowned National Negro Opera Company. Rahn also sang in the American opera *The Martyr* by Harry Freeman in 1947 and went on to create the lead in Jan Meyerowitz's opera *The Barrier* in 1950. Langston Hughes wrote the libretto. When *The Barrier* was given on Broadway, Rahn repeated her role singing opposite Lawrence Tibbett. From 1959 to 1960 she served as musical director for the German State Theatre production of *Bells are Ringing* in Frankfurt.

Muriel Rahn died on August 8, 1961, in New York City at the age of 50.

Sources

Obituary: *Musical America,* September 1961, 74.

Southern, Eileen, *Biographical Dictionary of Afro-American and African Musicians* (Westport, CT: Greenwood Press, 1982), 316.

"German Refugee, Ernest Kalibala to Broadcast," *New York Amsterdam News,* 4 March 1939, 17

The next Harlem Varieties Program, an exciting hour of news, music, drama and novelty sponsored by the Amsterdam News on Radio Station WHOM from 1 to 4 pm on Sundays, promises to be the most sparkling program yet presented in the series.

Under the skilled "emceeing" of clever Dick Campbell, whose talented wife, Muriel Rahn, is in charge of the opportunity hour, and with musical motif furnished by Buddy Walker's band, this program is fast becoming one of the most popular on the air.

Muriel Rahn with Jussi Bjoerling. Courtesy of the E. Azalia Hackley Collection, Detroit Public Library.

A glimpse at the unusually brilliant program set for Sunday, March 5, discloses the fact that Mrs. Lillian Sharpe Hunter will interview Ernest Kalibala, African scholar who is the principal and founder of the Aggrey Memorial School at Kampala, Uganda, which is called the "Tuskegee of Africa."

Others who are scheduled to appear include Adolph L. Morgens, German Negro who was forced to come to this country because of Hitler's Aryan policies, Mother Zion's choir, and the Regular Opportunity Hour under the direction of Miss Rahn.

"National Orchestral Association Enrolls Muriel Rahn, Soprano," *New York Amsterdam News,* 8 November 1941, 10

Selected from among over 250 applicants, all the others white, as a member of the Opera Group of the exclusive National Orchestral Association, Muriel Rahn, brilliant young dramatic soprano from Harlem, not only scored another Negro "first" this week but became a new colored operatic "find."

Miss Rahn, in private life, wife of Dick Campbell, noted actor, has been assigned roles in two operas, "Sister Angelica" and "Gianni Schicchi," both by Puccini; with otherwise all white casts, to be presented in Carnegie Hall next Spring. Her selection was based on possession of the best "operatic timbere" of voice, it was said.

The association furnishes opera and symphonic training to handpicked Americans from the best universities, conservatories, and music schools in the country, and after a period of apprenticeship, presents them in a series of operas at Carnegie Hall where they may be selected by impressarios and conductors for positions in the leading opera companies and symphony orchestras.

Miss Rahn's application, accepted only after endorsement by leading musical authorities and approved only after she had passed a rigid audition, including singing full roles of standard operas and singing at sight French, German and Italian songs before a musical board, entitles her to training free under Leon Barzin, musical director of the association, with rehearsals thrice weekly at Carnegie Hall.

A graduate of the Conservatory of the University of Nebraska and former teacher of music in several Negro colleges, Miss Rahn has arranged for time off from the Association's training schedule to fill her regular concert engagements, her next one slated for November 15 in the auditorium of Armstrong High School, Washington D.C.

"Young Violinist Gets Big Moment," *New York News,* 8 April 1944 (originally beneath a photo)

Everett Lee, young violinist in the *Carmen Jones* orchestra, received his big moment last week when he was chosen to conduct the orchestra after illness forced the regular conductor to be out. Muriel Rahn, Carmen of the show, is shown presenting Mr. Lee with flowers and congratulating him on being the first colored man to conduct a Broadway symphonic orchestra. Napoleon Reed, who was Joe for the evening, is waiting his chance to present the young man with a bottle of rum.

"Muriel Rahn, April 6," *Musical America,* 15 April 1947, 10

Muriel Rahn, soprano, who sang the leading role in *Carmen Jones,* appeared in recital in Town Hall accompanied by Melvin C. Owens. Miss Rahn's program encompassed arias by Handel and Verdi, German Lieder of Wolf and Schubert, a French group, contemporary songs and Negro Spirituals. Miss Rahn's voice has a fresh and opulent quality, but often her tones were forced and deviated from pitch. It would seem that at present the soprano's talents are more suited for the musical productions in the theatre than for appearances on the concert stage. With proper focusing of her natural gifts, however, it is possible that she may attain the status for which she seems to be aiming.

"Miss Rahn to Town Hall," *New York Amsterdam News,* 1 February 1958, 29

Muriel Rahn, versatile concert and opera soprano, will give her fourth New York Town Hall recital on Sunday, Feb. 16 at 8:30 p.m.

Miss Rahn made her debut in Town Hall in 1945 after singing the title role in "Carmen Jones" for a full season on Broadway. Subsequently, her career has embraced coast to coast concert tours annually as well as singing the title roles in the operas "Aida," "Salome" and "Cavalleria."

Miss Rahn's Town Hall programs, which in the past have always included an abundance of Negro composers, will be broadened on this occasion to cover a range of international contemporary composers. She will thus interpret musical works in five different languages.

In addition, she will introduce to the Town Hall audience the Margaret Bonds Chamber Music Ensemble which will accompany her on selections by Bach, Purcell and Gluck.

The Ensemble is composed of George DaCosta, 1st Violin, Clarence Render, 2nd Violin, Howard Rollock, Violist, Marion Cumbo, Cellist and Miss Bonds. Pianist Paul Meyer will accompany Miss Rahn on all other selections.

"Miss Rahn Pleases Town Hall Audience," *New York Amsterdam News,* 1 March 1958, 11

Muriel Rahn, concert and operatic soprano, thrilled a large and appreciative audience when she sang a diversified program at Town Hall Sunday evening.

The program opened with, "Hail Sabbath Day" by Bach, "Man Is for Woman Made" by Purcell and the well known "Divinities du Styx" from "Alceste" by Gluck.

Miss Rahn, who is an artist of first rank, won her audience from the first line of her group and held them to the end of the program at which time she had to sing four encores.

The artist sang songs in French, German and English.

Miss Rahn, who has always set a pattern, did an unusual thing. She devoted most of her program to English songs by modern composers many of whom were in the audience and stood after the singer and presented their music.

Few leading artists would attempt to sing this type of program; first, because singing in English is difficult and second most singers don't like to sing music of modern composers.

In speaking to this artist she said, "Some one must sing this music or it will never become known."

Music presented was by Paul Sargent, Reginald Boardman, Fela Sowande, Leonard Bernstein, Francis Reckling, W.C. Handy, Hall Johnson, Margaret Bonds and Sam Ralphing.

Little more can be said about Muriel Rahn as an artist since critics throughout the country and abroad have given her rave notices as concert artist and operatic soprano. Sunday evening merely added to her past praise.

The voice was full, the tones were beautifully sung, the voice line legato and the projection was such that you could hear every note to the smallest tone.

She sang the difficult Salome's address to the head of "Salome" by Strauss. Here the soprano displayed her ability to sing and interpret dramatic music. Bravo to this fine artist.

The Margaret Bonds chamber music ensemble with George DaCosta, Clarence Render, Howard Rollock, and Marion Cumbo shared in the program. Paul Meyer was at the piano.

"Miss Rahn Directs Success in Germany," *New York Amsterdam News,* 9 January 1960, 14

Frankfurt, Germany — Muriel Rahn, noted concert, opera and musical comedy star who was recently appointed Musical Director of the Stadtische Buhnen Theatre's all–German production of "Bells are Ringin," received glowing reviews of her work with the German cast this week when the show opened for a season's run.

The musical has been placed in the theatre's repertory and will alternate with other productions, as is customary in the German State Theatres. It will be presented on an average of four times weekly for the remainder of the season.

Miss Rahn will return to America next month for business and TV engagements. During the year, she has appeared in concerts and opera engagements in Germany, Italy, Yugoslavia, France, England and Austria.

LaJulia Rhea
(c. 1908–)

I didn't meet her until I went to college. Each year LaJulia Rhea gives an afternoon tea. She was the first black woman [for which] opera was of importance throughout her travels. Elegant woman. Everything in her home is done in gold and white. She maintains this house like it was in the Victorian Era and just lives in that world completely.

Charming woman. An era of the great prima donnas, the Melbas, etc. She's right in that kind of thing.

— *William Warfield, April 21, 1994*

When soprano LaJulia Rhea first heard the great African American soprano Florence Cole Talbert, during her high school days, she was inspired to pursue a career in opera.

She was born on March 16, ca. 1908, in Louisville, Kentucky. At the age of five she began studying the piano, and as a child sang in her aunt's church choir. At the age of sixteen her family moved to Chicago, Illinois, where she continued her musical training. In Chicago she studied at the National University of Music, directed by Pauline James Lee, and received her certificate in 1927 from the Chicago Musical College. Numbered among her voice teachers are Victor Chesnais, Herman DeVries, and Florence Cole Talbert. In 1927 she sang for the annual meeting of the National Association of Negro Musicians (NANM) in St. Louis, Missouri, and continued giving recitals throughout that period.

After developing an operatic and concert repertoire, LaJulia Rhea made her debut as a soprano in 1929 at Kimball Hall in Chicago. The Broadway musical *Rhapsody in Black* followed in 1931. Rhea sang a leading role and shared the stage with Ethel Waters and the Cecil Mack Choir. She had the historic opportunity to audition for the Metropolitan Opera Company in 1934, but was unable to overcome the Mets' racial policy. The honor of breaking down these racial barriers went to Marian Anderson, whom the Metropolitan engaged in 1955 as the Mets' first African American performer. Rhea toured the United States in 1935 after placing first in a Major Bowes radio talent show and landing a leading role in his amateur Ensemble Group, no. 2. Her operatic debut finally arrived in 1937. With William Franklin as Amonasro, LaJulia Rhea sang the title role in Verdi's *Aida* with the Chicago Civic Opera Company. Additional operas and operettas followed, including *Aida* once again in 1941. The occasion was the debut of Mary Cardwell Dawson's National Negro Opera Company in Pittsburgh, Pennsylvania.

SOURCES

Southern, Eileen, *Biographical Dictionary of Afro-American and African Musicians* (Westport, CT: Greenwood Press, 1982), 319–320.

William Howard Richardson
(1869–c1930s)

William Richardson, baritone, was born on August 23, 1869, in Liverpool, Nova Scotia. His paternal grandfather, a professional singer, led a concert company that consisted of his two daughters and three additional musicians. At age eleven his family moved to Boston. Richardson would begin his formal musical training there. One of his first voice teachers was George H. Woods, with whom Richardson made considerable progress. He made his first major recital appearance on April 20, 1909, at Boston's Steinert Hall. He then traveled to various cities appearing as baritone soloist in oratorios and concert works, including Samuel Coleridge-Taylor's Hiawatha trilogy. In 1913 he toured, with Maud Cuney-Hare, throughout the north and south on a lecture/recital tour. When he returned to Boston he studied with Arthur Hubbard, the noted voice teacher of Roland Hayes. Richardson also studied with Theodore Schroeder. In the summer of 1915 he toured with Roland Hayes, tenor, and William Lawrence, pianist, as part of the Hayes Trio. On January 30, 1919, he debuted in recital at Boston's Jordan Hall. He appeared in Cuba in 1923 after finishing a transcontinental tour of the cities from the Atlantic to the Pacific. He toured the Virgin Islands and Puerto Rico in 1923. He also appeared as the featured soloist with the San Juan Symphony Orchestra.

SOURCES

Cuney-Hare, Maud, *Negro Musicians and Their Music* (Washington, D.C.: Da Capo Press, 1936), 364–367.
Lovinggood, P.: *Famous Modern Negro Musicians* (New York, N.Y.: Press Forum Co., 1921/R1978), 41–43.
Southern, Eileen, *Biographical Dictionary of Afro-American and African Musicians* (Westport, CT: Greenwood Press, 1982), 320.

Paul Robeson
(1898–1976)

Paul Robeson was a true "Renaissance Man." He played fullback for his school football team, studied voice, acted on stage and screen, studied law and was politically active. He was born in Princeton, New Jersey, on April 9, 1898. Robeson entered Rutgers University in 1915. He was selected for the Phi Beta Kappa national honor society, won 15 sports honors, was twice named a Collegiate All-American in football, and was chosen as class valedictorian. He then attended Columbia University in New York as a law student. Prior to graduating in 1923 he continued playing football and participating in stage productions. He starred in two plays by Eugene O'Neill, *The Emperor Jones* and *All God's Chillun Got Wings.* He made his first film, *Body and Soul,* in 1924. In 1929 he added vocal recitals to his stage and film work. His repertoire consisted of primarily spirituals and international folk songs. His embrace of elements of Soviet philosophy and traditions, coupled with his civil rights activities, hurt his career greatly. He was blacklisted and his passport was revoked. He regained his passport in 1958 and performed once again until illness stopped his career. He died on January 23, 1976, from complications from a minor stroke. Robeson had a deep bass voice with a rare richness.

SOURCES

Abdul, Raoul, *Blacks in Classical Music: A Personal History* (New York: Dodd, Mead, 1978).
Hitchcock, H. Wiley, and Stanley Sadie, eds., *The New Grove Dictionary of American Music* (London: Macmillan, 1986).

Marie Selika
(1849–1937)

Mme. Marie Selika (Mrs. Sampson Williams) was one of the greatest African American concert singers of her day. The soprano took her stage name, Selika, from the heroine of the same name in the opera *L'Africaine* by Meyerbeer. At the insistence of Frances Bailey Gaskin, Mme.

Selika went to Boston where she stayed at the home of Gaskin's mother and continued her studies. She became proficient in German, Italian, and French. Lieutenant Dupree, a gentleman who managed and encouraged numerous young struggling African American artists, managed Mme. Selika. Upon her visit to Europe with her husband, an aspiring baritone, Mme. Selika achieved tremendous success. Mme. Selika and her husband eventually settled in Philadelphia, Pennsylvania. She apparently wished to perform jointly with her husband on her concerts. He was known as a man with a pleasant disposition and fine stage presence. However, his voice was said to be considerably inferior to hers, and as a result she often lost her chance at many quality performance opportunities. After her husband's death, Mme. Selika went to New York and taught voice at the Martin-Smith School of Music in Harlem. She died in 1937.

SOURCES

Obituary: *The Black Perspective in Music,* Vol. 13, No. 2, 244.

"Madame Selika Abroad — What Our Brilliant Lyric Artist Is Doing," *The New York Globe,* 3 March 1883

Boston, Feb. 26, — Much time having elapsed since the publication of our last account of the brilliant lyric artist Madame Selika — which account detailed her highly successful London debut at St. James Hall, October 14 last — it is quite probable that her many American admirers will be interested in learning of her subsequent progress. In a former article reference was made to the great hosts of musical and theatrical people, many of them artists of the finest ability, who are constantly and well nigh desperately vying with each other for a hearing before the great London public. Of course only a few, comparatively, of this legion of contestants can succeed in making a public appearance and therefore many are glad of a chance to gain a mere foothold by charging nothing for their services at concerts, etc. Indeed many quite fair artists even pay managers for what is called the privilege of appearing, while all the time, as before mentioned, the artistic (?) rivalry is something fearful to contemplate. Entering then, this already over-crowded and by no means inferior field of musical people, it will be seen how very great are the difficulties with which from the very first, our stranger cantatrice had to contend. Yet equipped with that rather sweet voice (the predominating charms of which Mr. Strakosch has already warmly declared are "rarely to be found outside of Italy"), captivatingly naive, courageous, and with other valuable accessories of the success-winning artist, Madame Selika ere long won a London hearing and made the remarkable debut already described.

Previous to this and afterward, about six months in all were devoted to study and practice under Signor Mazzoni — with occasional public appearances — all with fine results.

Since then, Mme. Selika has been the chief attraction at concerts in Scotland and Germany, in the meantime declining, for good reasons, one or two fine offers to return soon to America with concert troupes, composed of excellent English artists. At last advices she was singing at the "Musee Du Nord," Brussels, Belgium, and had under consideration an offer for an engagement at Munchen, Bavaria.

Madame Selika had previously sung in France. Mr. Williams writes that there is much adverse feeling in Paris towards colored people since the Zulus slew Prince Napoleon — that is, among the rich and aristocratic class, who, he says, are generally monarchists. He describes Brussels as a charmingly beautiful city, calling it "the miniature Paris." Here, as elsewhere in the line of their travels, himself and Madame Selika have never once been slighted on account of their color and at the most elegantly appointed hotel in Brussels they could not have received more polite attention had they been Madame Patti and husband. What a lesson for our yet uncivilized America! Only one colored person was seen at Brussels, and he came and went perfectly unconscious of any difference in his complexion or of remark from, or isolation by, his fairer skinned fellow citizens — for from none of these rather inconvenient things did he suffer in the least. While boarding the steamer for Brussels, Mr. Williams accidentally dropped overboard his satchel containing unanswered letters from American friends and some valued addresses. Their friends are requested as far as possible to renew the lost correspondence, addressing Madame Selika and husband, care of the American Exchange, 449 Strand, London, England from whence all letters will be forwarded to the addresses.

The "Jubilee" business, once so flourishing there, has been over-done in England and Germany, write our friends and the people there want no more of it. This has been caused primarily by the bad, dishonest conduct of many members of the (genuine) jubilee troupes from America and afterwards by "burnt cork" (white) imitation in and from London. This we know was never said, nor would it ever be said, of our famous jubilee singers of Fisk University, ever unique and charming in their wonderful music, while also always winning the respect and everlasting friendship of strangers by their gentlemenlike and ladylike conduct both on and off the stage. Since their remarkable European tours, however, a number of stray troupes have crossed from America and with little or no vocal ability, but with much looseness of habits — amounting at times to lewdness on the part of female members — have so disgusted the English and German people as to have well nigh spoiled the excellent impression made by the "Fisk's" and, perhaps, one other credible troupe.

Madame Selika is profuse in her thanks to the prosperous brothers, Messrs Bohee, who were ever friendly and even devoted to herself and husband while the latter remained in London. These gentlemen (formerly from Chicago, I think) are still meeting with great success in their professions. In fact, they are now considered permanent London institutions. This shows what talent combined with study and luck can do. But this rather desultory account ought to soon close. During the stay abroad of Madame Selika, Mr. Sampson Williams, her husband, has acted as her manager, and has also assisted as baritone soloist and in duos at a number of her concerts. He also took lessons of Signor Mazzoni, and has improved a voice and method which all who heard him sing with her will readily admit were already good and artistic. And it may be truly and proudly said of both these our representatives in vocal art, that they have fairly won their way in distant lands by their excellent talents, which from the very first have been steadily accompanied and strengthened by the most assiduous pain-staking study. To these requisites of the successful artist, Madame Selika and Mr. Williams have, of course added that other quality which someone has strongly called "clear grit." May their sun of success continue to shine brightly.

It remains to be seen whether our much vaunting "musical race" in America will on the return of Madame Selika from Europe, with her high endorsements from the best judges there, whom a just feeling of pride in her latest achievements by attending in large numbers wherever she may sing, with a voice and method which although affording great delight before her departure will have been improved necessarily by studies and practice under one of the first masters of London, as well as by her observation and public performances in England, Scotland, France, Germany and Belgium. In such cities as Boston, New York, Philadelphia, Chicago, Baltimore, Cincinnati, Louisville, and others no hall or theatre ought to be large enough to contain all the colored people — to say nothing of the whites — who would flock to see her. We shall see, we shall see.

"Madame Marie Selika, Something of Her History and Success as a Vocalist — *Queen of Staccato*, She filled Madame Gerster's Place — Sang the Leading Role in L'Africaine — Her Success in Europe — Sings with Patti in London," *The Cleveland Gazette*, 28 April 1888

The colored race has produced many accomplished and talented women in the musical world, among whom are Miss Adelaide G. Smith, a highly cultured soprano; Madame Lavelle Jones, also a soprano; Mrs. Carrie Lucas (nee Melain), who is an expert manipulator of the violin, cornet, zither and xylophone; Madame V.A. Montgomery, an organist of a very high order; and a score of others. The two pioneers of all these are Mmes.

Marie Selika, prima donna soprano, and Nellie Brown Mitchell, an accomplished soprano, with a copious voice of great compass, remarkable purity and melody. Madame Selika, who has in every respect merited the title of "the Patti of the African race," has had more experience than any of her sister artists here mentioned. She was born in Natchez, Mississippi, in 1849 and was taken to Cincinnati when a child, where she remained until she arrived at womanhood, and where she first began to develop her wonderful natural vocal gift under local teachers. In 1873 or 1874 she went to San Francisco and studied under Signor Bianci, a great master of the vocal art and a famous operatic tenor. Returning east, she stopped and studied in Chicago one year with Signor Farini. After she came east, she made her appearance in concert and continued her studies, visiting Boston in 1878. An opportunity was afforded her that was not only pleasant and profitable to her, but an honour to the entire race to which she belongs. She filled Madame Gerster's place at a concert in Aeolian Hall, Boston, and subsequently sang the leading role in L'Africaine in the city at the Academy of Music. After making a successful tour through the East in concert, she gave a complimentary benefit at Boston Music Hall which was attended by Governor Long and his staff and other citizens of note of Massachusetts. In June 1882, she sailed for Europe, where she remained nearly four years. Her first year was spent in London, where she studied with Signor Mazoni, after which she went to Germany and sang in nearly all the large cities. She also sang in Russia, Denmark, Sweden, and Austria, and returned to America in 1885, since which time she has been appearing in concert. Madam Selika is particularly noted for her trills and staccatos, and it has been said by able critics that she only excelled as a prima donna soprano by Madame Adelina Patti and Signor Vergora in a concert for the benefit of the fund in aid of the Cuban Slave children, and under the patronage of the Marquis de Cuna Laiglesia. *The London Daily News*, in speaking of the artist, said Madame Selika fairly enraptured the immense audience that assembled at St. James' Hall. She sang two numbers—Dana's "Ave Maria" and the polka song, "Frior di Margherita." And, says the *News*; "each number was vociferously applauded." Madame Selika is now appearing in concert in the West,—Arneaux, in N.Y Sun [sic]. Madame Selika and her husband Sampson W. Williams, a baritone, sang recently in Cleveland, Ohio; Chicago, Illinois; and Louisville, Kentucky. Their home is in Columbus, Ohio.

"The Martin Recital," *The New York Age*, 30 April 1914, p. 6

The culmination of a year's successful endeavor came before a large and appreciative audience last Friday night at New Star Casino, when the music pupils of David Irwin Martin, director of the Music School Settlement for Colored People in the City of New York appeared in their seventh annual recital. Mr. Martin's pupils are mostly juveniles, with a few adults, but the program was entirely unlike that usually rendered by children. The pupils were assisted by the orchestra and chorus from the Music School Settlement and by the Riverdale Orphan Asylum chorus.

There were several members of special interest. Mme. Maria Selika, who has charmed audiences in all sections of this country and in Europe for many years, appeared on the program, assisted by the children of the Colored Orphan Asylum at Riverdale and the senior orchestra of the Music School Settlement, singing an arrangement by Bush of Foster's "Old Folks at Home."

George Shirley
(1934–)

George Irving Shirley holds the distinction of being the first African American tenor to sing with the Metropolitan Opera Company. He was born on April 18, 1934, in Indianapolis, Indiana. When his family relocated to Detroit, Michigan, he began studying music. While in Detroit he entered Wayne State University where he studied music education. In 1955 he received his bachelors degree. His career as a teacher was soon interrupted, for he was drafted the following year. Upon entering the military he became the first African American member of the United States Army Chorus. In 1959, after his discharge, he studied voice with Therny Georgi in Washington, D. C. and Cornelius Reid in New York. Shirley made his operatic debut with a small opera troupe, the Turnau Opera Players, in Woodstock, New York. He performed the role of Eisenstein in *Die Fledermaus*. In 1960 he sang the role of Rodolfo at the Teatro Nuovo, Milan, making his European debut. That same year he won the American Opera Auditions. The following year he made his debut in the same role with the New York City Opera and the San Francisco Opera. Also in 1961 Mr. Shirley won the prestigious Metropolitan Opera auditions and made his debut with that company on October 24, 1961, as Ferrando. He sang there until 1973. While at the Metropolitan Opera he sang 28 roles from 26 operas. These roles include Pinkerton, Alfredo, Don Ottavio, Romeo and Almaviva. He also sang at Spoleto, Santa Fe Covent Garden, Glyndebourne and La Scala in Milan. On April 14, 1977, he created the role of Romilayu in Kirchner's *Lily* with the New York City Opera. He taught at the University of Maryland and was named the Joseph Edgar Maddy Distinguished University Professor at the University of Michigan in 1992.

SOURCES

Abdul, Raoul, *Blacks in Classical Music: A Personal History* (New York: Dodd, Mead, 1978).

Smith, Eric Ledell. *Blacks in Opera: An Encyclopedia of People and Companies, 1873–1993* (Jefferson, N.C.: McFarland, 1994).

Hitchcock, H. Wiley, and Stanley Sadie, eds., *The New Grove Dictionary of American Music* (London: Macmillan, 1986).

Muriel Smith
(1923 or 1925–1985)

Muriel Smith was born on February 23 in New York City and died on September 13 in Richmond, Virginia. The Curtis Institute of Philadelphia was the site of her musical education, and she studied privately with Elizabeth Schumann. Smith alternated with noted soprano Muriel Rahn in the role of *Carmen Jones*, Oscar Hammerstein's version of Bizet's opera. In 1947 she left the cast and sang in other musicals, including *The Cradle Will Rock* by Marc Blitzstein. Settling in London in 1949, she sang in numerous musicals and operas throughout her years there. At Covent Garden she sang the title role in *Carmen*. Smith returned to the United States in 1970 and joined the voice faculty at Virginia Union University in 1974. In 1984 she received the Arts Award of the National Council of Negro Women.

SOURCES

Obituary: *The Black Perspective in Music*, Vol. 13, and No. 2, 244.

Theodore C. Stone
(–1998)

We go way back. The first time I met Theodore C. Stone…It would've been after I came out of the army and I was staying in a hotel called Hotel America. And as I was at the desk this very handsome man, with waves for days, stepped to the desk and started to talk…He models clothes and things like that…You name it he may have done it. I went to a concert [of his] with him once. He came out in an ordinary tuxedo. And I think the *Toreador Song* was the single piece on the program…I looked up and here came Stone out in full costume with hat on for the *Toreador Song*. And then the next half he came out in a gold tuxedo with a gold tie. This is typical of him. He became president of NANM (National Association of Negro Musicians) and was the man that was actually responsible for my joining the organization. He had me do a concert for, I think it was, the 16th anniversary. And he said, "Now you ought to belong to this organization." I was very impressed… Every year he was noted for giving a recital…Straight up to now. He was doing the standard repertoire: chanson, lieder, oratorio, opera arias. An excellent baritone, high baritone…his programs of these recent years have been more or less song literature as such, more than emphasizing opera. It wasn't as operatic a sound as Robert McFerrin. With Robert you'd have thought he was an Italian baritone, really schooled.

— *William Warfield, April 21, 1994*

"Fears Russians," *New York Amsterdam News,* 21 October 1939, 13

Theodore Charles Stone, American baritone, whose recent concert in Helsinki, Finland, was a tremendous success, is anxious to return home because of the fear that the Russians will soon take over Finland and that it will then be more difficult for him to get out of the country. Stone, whose home is in Chicago, sailed from New York in July to study under Kosti Vehanan, noted Finnish musician, and accompanist for Marian Anderson.

"Singer Is Back from Finland," *New York Amsterdam News,* 6 January 1940, 11

Theodore Charles Stone, concert baritone, arrived in New York Christmas Day on board the S.S. Astrid Thorden from Finland, bringing a breath-taking story of life under fire of Russian bombing in the beleaguered Finnish capital, Helsinki.

The only Negro known to have been in the tiny Baltic country when Joseph Stalin's battle-browed legions were hurled at the Mannerheim line, Mr. Stone's safe return to the United States will bring relief to hundreds of his friends in New York, Chicago, and his native Texas.

Stone narrowly escaped death from a bomb dropped from a Russian plane, which completely destroyed a large building just across the street from his apartment in Helsinki, two days after the war began. A total of 41 persons were killed in the bombardment, the singer declared.

"The Russians are doing much damage in their bombardments, but the Finnish people are holding the invading troops well in check," he stated.

"I'm glad to be back in America," he added "and I can say it is mighty good to be in America in a time like this."

Due to the danger of mines, the Astrid Thorden was required to use extra pilots and the utmost care to reach New York. A few hours before the Thorden reached the most dangerous part of the North Sea, Stone stated, one Swedish ship was sunk and two days later a Finnish ship ran into a mine in the same part of the sea.

Stone had been studying and singing while in Finland, and in Helsinki he said he met the great Finnish composer Jean Sibelius, as well as Seleim Palmgren, Kauka Ero and Heini Leinaska. The countries Stone went to are Sweden, Norway, and Denmark, as well as Estonia and Russia. Encouragement received from Kosti Vehanen, accompanist for Marian Anderson, led Stone to make the trip to Finland.

"Theodore Stone Is Auditioned for White House," *New York Amsterdam News,* 17 February 1940, 11

Theodore Charles Stone, the young concert artist who returned recently from the war zone in Helsinki, Finland, has been auditioned for a possible appearance at the White House in Washington; it was learned this week. Preparations for the recital started several weeks ago when Mrs. Franklin D. Roosevelt announced her social event plans for the spring season.

Mr. Stone, a Chicagoan, was one of the few Americans in Helsinki at the outbreak of the war. While there he studied under one of the leading musicians in Europe. In the event of a White House appearance, the baritone soloist will probably be added to the list of such celebrated artists as Lawrence Tibbett and Marian Anderson.

"Singer, Pianist Appear Jointly," *New York Amsterdam News,* 8 June 1940, 17

Appearing in joint recital before an appreciative audience at Baha'i Center, 119 West 57th Street, Sunday, Theodore Charles Stone, baritone, and Margaret Bonds, pianist, won praise for their performances.

The occasion marked Stone's fourth and Miss Bond's first formal recital in this city. The singer offered a varied program, including works of the best-known composers, native Finnish songs and Negro spirituals. Miss Bonds, besides accompanying Stone, played selections from Bach, Brahms, Coleridge-Taylor, and a number of her own compositions.

Florence Cole Talbert
(c. 1890–1961)

Florence Cole Talbert was born in Detroit, Michigan. She eventually moved to Los Angeles, California, where she received her first musical education at the University of California. After three seasons of traveling she continued her studies at the Chicago Musical College. Upon her graduation she was awarded the diamond medal and the added opportunity of performing with the Chicago Symphony Orchestra at the commencement exercises. She chose *Caro Nome* from Verdi's *Rigoletto* as her commencement selection. A touring period with the Hahn Singers, and numerous song recitals soon followed. Talbert then decided to continue her vocal training in New York with Oscar Saenger. Saenger once commented, "Her voice is a beautiful soprano, which she uses with consummate skill. This, combined with splendid musicianship, places her in the front rank of artists."

Talbert's next vocal instructor was Delia Valeri of Italy. While in Italy she sang the title role in Verdi's *Aida*. She continued her concert career, returning to the United States in 1929.

Florence Talbert died in 1961.

SOURCES

Cuney-Hare, Maud, *Negro Musicians and Their Music* (Washington, D.C.: Da Capo Press, 1936), 368–369.
Lovinggood, P., *Famous Modern Negro Musicians* (New York, N.Y.: Press Forum co., 921/R197), 31–33.

Fred Thomas

Fred Thomas I think was one of the first black winners of the Metropolitan Opera auditions. I got to know Fred Thomas because in *Call Me Mister*, Fred Thomas was my understudy. And we got to be friends, and that was in 1952 and we've remained friends ever since.

He's the treasurer of the National Association of Negro Musicians now. He's been for several years and we see each other frequently. Always in August at the convention Fred is there handling those books. And don't allow nobody to mess with him either. "I've been doin' this for forty years and I know it has to be done this way!"

— *William Warfield, April 21, 1994*

"Fred Thomas with N.Y. Opera Theatre," *New York Amsterdam News,* **23 January 1960, 13**

Fred Thomas, bass baritone, will star with the New York Opera Theatre in its opening presentation, Gounod's "Romeo et Juliette" sung in French.

Under the direction of James Lucas the French opera will be held at Master Institute Theatre 310 Riverside Drive on Tuesday, Jan. 26 and Wednesday, Jan. 27 with the curtain rising promptly at 8:15.

Mr. Thomas has the role of the father of Juliette and is the only tan soloist in this opera with the New York Opera Theatre.

Shirley Verrett
(1931–)

Shirley Verrett was born in New Orleans, Louisiana, on May 31, 1931. She began her career as a mezzo-soprano and later added soprano roles to her repertoire. Her father, a Seventh-Day Adventist church choir director, gave Verrett her initial vocal instruction. She would eventually study with two giants of opera of the early twentieth century, Lotte Lehmann and John Charles Thomas. She won the Marian Anderson Award in 1955 and a scholarship to the famous Juilliard School of Music in New York. While there, she studied with Marion Szekely-Freschi. Her operatic debut took place in Yellow Springs, Ohio, in 1957 as Benjamin Britten's Lucretia. She joined the New York City Opera Company in 1958 and made her European debut the following year in Cologne as the Gypsy in *Rasputin's End* by Nabokov. In 1960, while still a student, she appeared as soloist in Falla's *El amor brujo* under the baton of Leopold Stokowski. The following decade brought debuts at Spoleto, the Bolshoi Theater in Moscow, Milan' La Scala, the Metropolitan Opera in 1968 and Covent Garden. Her vast array of roles includes Amneris, Eboli, Ulrica, Norma, Delilah, Dido, Cassandra, Lady Macbeth, Tosca and Aida.

SOURCES

Abdul, Raoul, *Blacks in Classical Music: A Personal History* (New York: Dodd, Mead, 1978).

Hitchcock, H. Wiley, and Stanley Sadie, eds., *The New Grove Dictionary of American Music* (London: Macmillan, 1986).

Jenkins, S., "Shirley Verrett," *Opera, xxiv* (1973), 585–9.

Smith, Eric Ledell, *Blacks in Opera: An Encyclopedia of People and Companies, 1873–1993* (Jefferson, N.C.: McFarland, 1994).

Steane, J. B., *The Grand Tradition* (London, 1974), 418–19.

Rachael Walker
(c. 1873–c. 1940s)

Soprano Rachael Walker was most likely born in Cleveland, Ohio. While in Cleveland she studied with John Underner. By 1886 she was appearing on local concerts as a concert soprano and as a pianist. Prior to embarking on a professional concert career, she taught in the public schools of Cleveland in the early 1890s. During the mid–1890s she appeared with the Midnight Star Concert Company (later called the Ednorah Nahor Concert Company) and with a company sponsored by the Henry Wolfson Musical Bureau. She toured California with the latter organization. In 1895 she went to New York and sang the following year at Hammerstein's Olympic Roof Garden. As a result, she was dubbed "the Creole Nightingale" and commanded management of the highest calibre. In 1897 she went to England and remained there for eighteen years. Walker appeared at the Pavillion Theatre in London and sang for the Queen of Spain, the Princess of Saxe-Coburg and Gotha, and many more. She achieved the admiration of the French composers Jules Massenet and Camille Saint-Saens, and studied with Sir Henry J. Wood of England. World War I brought her back to the United States by 1915. Rachael Walker eventually settled in Cleveland once again, remaining there until her death.

SOURCES

Cuney-Hare, Maud, *Negro Musicians and Their Music* (Washington, D.C.: Da Capo Press, 1936), 233–234.

Southern, Eileen, *Biographical Dictionary of Afro-American and African Musicians* (Westport, CT: Greenwood Press, 1982), 387–388.

The *[Indianapolis] Freeman*, 26 September 1896

Miss Rachel Walker of Cleveland, Ohio, who by the way, is billed as the "Creole Nightingale," has been singing at Hammerstein's Olympia Roof

Garden, New York City, for the past several weeks. The *New York Dramatic News*, one of the leading theatre papers, recently had the following to say editorially of Miss Walker:

"It is seldom that a singer of such real artistic worth as Rachel Walker is heard at a roof garden, but that such merit is appreciated by Olympia patrons is attested by the storms of applause which nightly reward that artist's efforts. Miss Walker is a Creole about 23 years of age, and possesses a mezzo-soprano voice of rare beauty and flexibility. She sings with the intensity and appreciation of a real artist, and her talents entitle her to high rank on the concert stage, for hers is not merely a finely trained voice without a trace of personality, but one full of expression and appreciation of the composer's idea. Her first song was evidently a vocal arrangement of a violin solo, familiar to the concert goer, which enabled her to show her technique, but for her remaining songs she wisely dropped the severely classical and gave 'The Last Rose of Summer' and 'Swanee River,' to the unbounded satisfaction of the audience."

The [Indianapolis] Freeman, 24 October 1896

Miss Rachel Walker has signed a contract with Mr. Hammerstein, the vaudeville king, to sing in the principal cities of the country. Her engagement with Mr. Hammerstein is for 25 weeks, and at the close she will return to the Paris conservatory to complete her studies.

William Caesar Warfield
(1920–2002)

Hailed throughout the world as one of the great vocal artists of the second half of the twentieth century, William Warfield mastered every field open to a singer's art. His New York Town Hall debut on March 19, 1950, pushed him overnight into the front ranks of concert artists. After his remarkable debut his career flourished in many artistic areas. In 1950 he was invited by the Australian Broadcasting Commission to tour that continent for 35 concerts, including solo performances with their five leading symphony orchestras. During that tour his manager, Larney Goodkind, signed a contract with Metro-Goldwyn-Mayer (MGM) for Warfield to play the featured role of Joe in the 1951 film version of Jerome Kern's musical *Showboat*. It was Hollywood's biggest box-office success of the year. The worldwide exhibition of the film resulted in the worldwide demand for Warfield. During the first few days of the film's production, Johnny Green, the MGM studio orchestra conductor, suggested that Warfield "run-through" the song "Old Man River" once to give him an idea of timing and balances preliminary to actual production. When they played back the tape, the conductor, director, and producer were so startled by the result that they immediately sent for the head of MGM, Louis B. Mayer, to come hear the tape for himself. After hearing it, the movie mogul wiped his tearing eyes. Singers were not expected to complete their task in one take. The procedure had always been to record a song many times and then splice the best phrases together for the finished product. In the case of Warfield the "run-through" became the finished product. He also sang in stage productions of *Show Boat* for the Vienna Volksoper in 1966, and from 1971 to 1972.

William Warfield was born in West Helena, Arkansas, on January 22, 1920, the eldest of five sons. While William was still a small child, his father decided to move his family to Rochester, New York. In 1942 William received his Bachelor of Music degree from the Eastman School of Music in Rochester. During the Second World War Warfield served in Military Intelligence in the War Department due to his proficiency in foreign languages. After serving, he studied with Otto Herz, Yves Tinaure, and Rosa Ponselle. In 1947 he was engaged for the singing lead in the national touring company of the Broadway hit *Call Me Mister*. Three other members of the cast went on to achieve success, as did Warfield: Comedian Buddy Hackett, comedian and writer Carl Reiner, and choreographer-dancer-director Robert Fosse. He has made six tours for the United States State Department, more than any other American solo artist has. In 1958 his performance schedule required two trips around the world in order to give concerts in nine countries of Asia, including Vietnam, Cambodia and Laos, a solo recital in Brussels for the Belgian World's Fair, 40 concerts for his second Australian tour, and 25 concerts in the United States. He was also the first American solo artist to cover the African continent.

In the early 1950s Warfield introduced Aaron Copland's settings of *Old American Songs*. Since that time he recorded two versions of the songs, one with Aaron Copland accompanying at the piano and an orchestral version with Aaron Copland conducting. Warfield's most famous stage role was the title role in George Gershwin's opera *Porgy and Bess*. He appeared in numerous productions of the work, including the 1952–1953 revival in the United States and Europe, 1961 and 1964 in New York, and 1965–1972 at the Vienna Volksoper in Austria. In 1957 and 1959 Warfield played the speaking role of "De Lawd" in Marc Connelly's play *The Green Pastures* for NBC-TV's *Hallmark Hall of Fame*. Throughout his career

William Warfield appearing on an episode of the television show *Over Easy* (1980). Photographs and Prints Division, Schomburg Center for Research in Black Culture, The New York Public Library, Astor, Lenox and Tilden Foundations.

Warfield has appeared on many radio and television programs, being presented by Eddie Cantor, Edger Bergen, Ed Sullivan, Kate Smith, Milton Berle, *The Bell Telephone Hour*, *The Voice of Firestone*, *Lux Theatre*, and others.

In March of 1984 he received a Grammy Award for his spoken performance in Aaron Copland's *A Lincoln Portrait*. From 1972 to 1990 he served as a member of the voice faculty, and eventually its chairman at the University of Illinois. From 1952 to 1972 he was married to the renowned soprano Leontyne Price.

SOURCES

Conversation with William Warfield, April 21, 1994, Brainerd, Minnesota.
De Lerma, Dominique-René, *The New Grove Dictionary of American Music* (New York: St. Martin's Press, 1986), Vol. 4, 477.
Southern, Eileen, *Biographical Dictionary of Afro-American and African Musicians* (Westport, CT: Greenwood Press, 1982), 391.

"William Warfield, Baritone, Town Hall, March 19, 3:00 (Debut)," *Musical America*, April 1950, 18

It is especially delightful to welcome a new recital artist when he comes to public attention virtually unknown. Mr. Warfield's debut was the more impressive for qualities hitherto unrevealed in several Broadway assignments, the latest of which was as Cal in Marc Blitestein Regina. The Negro singer has, since his discharge from the Army, studied only a short time at the Eastman School and with the American Theatre Wing, and has worked in nightclubs to make a living. The fruit of his work was apparent in a rich program, sumptuously sung.

There is no facet of the singer's art missing from Mr. Warfield's equipment. First of all, he possesses a voice of great beauty and flexibility. His technical equipment includes a command of breath that enables him to spin out a tone to exquisite fineness; steadiness of support equal to the demands of every work he sang; a good trill (extraordinary, indeed, among male singers); and an even production throughout an uncommonly wide range. Yet all of these attributes seemed merely servants to the artistic purpose that pervaded everything he sang. In fact, the listener was prone to forget all technical considerations in the wealth of stylistic variety, which was one of the singer's most notable assets.

This sure sense of style revealed its many sides as the afternoon progressed. Equally at ease in the disparate worlds of oratorio, spirituals, lieder, and French art songs, he brought to each its own coloration and a perceptive penetration into the meaning of texts. His opening group, called Songs of the Believer, included religious music by Schutz, Perotin, Handel, and Monteverdi, as well as traditional spirituals. Particularly fine were the flawless ornaments of Monteverdi's "Laudate Dominum" in *Sanctus Ejus*, and the effortless negotiation of florid passages in "Thy glorious deeds inspired my tongue," from Handel's *Samson*.

In the Schubert and Loewe lieder that followed, moods ranged from gay to grave, and each found its proper projection in the baritone's interpretations. On the arrival of Faure's La Bonne Chanson, nine songs to poems by Verlaine, an enthralled audience witnessed another transformation. In this cycle, which demands a wide range of expression, he exhibited sensitivity of high order, lyric tenderness, and beautiful tone color.

An American group that included three new works demonstrated that Mr. Warfield sang his native tongue with as impressively good diction as he had displayed in the art works of other lands. Sam Raphling's "Homesick Blues," to a poem by Langston Hughes; Ernst Bacon's setting of Carl Sandburg's "Brady"; and John Klein's narrative ballad, "The Ledo Road," to a poem by Smith Dawless, were given first performances. Mr Warfield also sang Marion Bauer's "The Minstrel of Romance," Howard Swanson's "The Negro Speaks of Rivers," and Paul Bowles' "Cabin." He won his audience in this group as in others, and they summoned him back for two encores—"Jubilee Shouts," in which he replaced his accompanist, Otto Herz, at the piano. Throughout the afternoon, Mr. Herz supplied accompaniments of rare sensibility.

"William Warfield, Baritone Town Hall, Jan 28," *Musical America,* February 1951, 244

William Warfield, whose recital debut last season was so startling a success, returned to give his second New York recital after having completed a strenuous and extremely successful tour of Australia. A near capacity audience was on hand to greet him and acclaim everything he did.

A large, affable young man with an ingratiating simplicity of deportment on the stage, Mr. Warfield offered an intelligently devised program, in which standard items were mingled with those by relatively unfamiliar composers, and fresh choices form the works of familiar ones. Perhaps the most impressive thing about his recital was the native flair he showed for winning his audience and holding their attention without ever compromising the integrity of his art. His musicianship was extraordinarily good, his intellectual mastery of his program complete, and his diction — in English, French, and German — above reproach.

Beginning with Andreas Hammerschmidt's motet De Profundis, Mr. Warfield continued with Oh, Sleep! Why dost thou leave me? from Handel's Semele; Good fellows, be merry from Bach's Peasant Cantata; and Oh God! Have mercy, from Mendelssohn's St. Paul. His voice warmed up slowly, perhaps because of his recent tiring schedule, and in this group its considerable natural beauty was marred by a good number of unfocused tones, by a tremolo, and, particularly in the Bach aria, by a sense of strain in forte top tones.

A German group followed—Loewe's Des Glockthurmers Tochterlein and Hochzeitlied and Wolf's Fusseise; Nun Wandre, Maria; and Trunken mussen wir Allen Sein. Here Mr. Warfield lightened his production markedly, phrased with unexceptionable taste, and met the interpretative demands as completely as could be wished, although a certain lack of clarity in his tones was still noticeable.

In the ensuing French group — Pierre de Breville's Venise Marine and Le Furet du Bois Joli, and Debussy's Le Son du Cor d'Afflige, L'echelonnement des Haise, Ballade pour Prier Notre-Dame, and Ballade des Femmes de Paris— he lightened his voice still further, and achieved some very beautiful piano and mezzavoce effects. The only criticism that could be offered is that the De Breville songs, insipid in their vague impressionism, were hardly worth the singer's talents.

A final group of American songs included the first American performance of Aaron Copland's set of five Old American Songs, which includes a lovely sentimental ballad, A Long Time Ago, and the Shaker song Simple Gifts. Copland has refrained from dressing the material up, and the result is a charming little set of songs with impeccably tasteful accompaniments. There was also the first performance anywhere of Howard Swanson's Cahoots, and the same composer's Joy. The new Swanson song is hardly his best, and the text is no better than third rate Carl Sandburg.

"William Warfield on Radio, May 12,"
Chicago Defender, 10 May 1958, 15

William Warfield, noted American baritone, will be guest soloist on the Monday, May 12, broadcast of The Telephone Hour (NBC Radio, 9 pm, EDT), with Donald Voorhees and Bell Telephone Orchestra. WMAQ is the Chicago outlet.

Mr. Warfield's opening group will be made up of two songs by Robert Schumann, "Im Wunderschoenen Monat Mai" and "Ich Grolle Nicht." In his second group he will sing two traditional spirituals, the Burleigh arrangement of "Go Down Moses" and the Hall Johnson arrangement of "Ride on, King Jesus." His final selection on the program will be the aria "Infelice e tu credevi" from Verdi's "Ernani."

Naomi Watson

"Naomi Watson, Contralto (Debut),"
Musical America, 12 May 1945, 12

Naomi Watson, Negro contralto from Quincy, Ill, made a New York debut at the Town Hall on April 22. She undertook an elaborate program beginning with old Italian airs by Durante, Marcello and Rossi, Shubert's "Du bist die Ruh," Brahms's "Wie Melodien," Henschel's "Morning Hymn," Faure's "Les Berceaux," and "Amour viens aider" aria from "Samson and Delilah," songs by Gretchaninoff, Mednikoff, Mussorgsky, MacDowell, a group of Spirituals and other matters.

Miss Watson ought to be a more satisfying artist, for she is gifted with a voice of fine quality and rich texture, copious in volume and wide in range. If she showed no profound gifts of emotional insight she is nevertheless a singer of serious purpose and manifest intelligence, earnestness and dignity. All the more regrettable are those faults of technique that prevent her realizing the effects, which ought to be easily within her grasp. Miss Watson appears never to have acquired a correct method of breathing and support. Her tones throughout the scale are afflicted with an incessant tremolo and their production results in prevailing spread and "edgy" sounds. Nor is it surprising that her pitch is sometimes decidedly insecure.

With proper schooling, Miss Watson ought to be a singer considerably above the average. Her performance of the Saint-Saens aria, for one thing, disclosed an unmistakable sensitiveness for operatic style. But her diction, particularly her treatment of French, leaves much to be desired. Arpad Sandor was her accompanist. A numerous audience received her cordially.

"Naomi Watson, Contralto," *Musical America,* October 1947, 17

Naomi Watson, contralto, who has sung previously in Town Hall, gave a recital there on the afternoon of September 20, with Arpad Sandor at the piano. Miss Watson again made a good impression, both by the quality of her voice and by her interpretive ability. There was, at times, an unnecessary vibrato, but in general her production was satisfactory. Arias by Bach and Handel were well done. In the second group in German, there was some irregularity of presentation. Die Junge Nonne is not a difficult song, nor is Brahms' Botschaft, the latter, especially, with a good pianist in attendance. Franck's La Procession, however, requires something more than Miss Watson brought to it. Fourdrain's Carnaval was a part of this group. The somewhat banal aria from Tchaikovsky's Jeanne d'Arc showed the singer's vocal abilities to an agreeable extent. A group in English by American and British composers followed and the program ended with the inevitable Spirituals.

Portia White

Musical America, 25 December 1945, 11

Portia White, Negro contralto from Novia Scotia, made another recital appearance at Town Hall Dec. 5 before a sizable audience. Her program ranged through Lieder by Schubert and Brahms, French songs by Szulc, Bizet, Faure, Fourdrain, the "O mio Fernando" aria from *La Favorita* and a group of folksongs. Fredrerick Kitzinger was her accompanist.

Miss White's voice is a naturally excellent organ but rather uneven in its technical schooling. There are tones of real opulence in the middle of the scale, particularly round and vital when delivered with full power. In such cases it seems true operatic material and so she was able to give the Donizetti air with considerably more punch and impact than her Schubert or her French numbers. Those offerings, earnestly as Miss White addressed herself to them, fell somewhat short in point of style and interpretative insight.

Camilla Williams
(1922–)

Camilla Williams I got to know a little better because Camilla I met early in her career too. And Camilla is *the* prima donna. She lives, breathes, and is the essence of what a prima donna should be. She wears turbans and she has a turban that fits every outfit that she wears. She wouldn't be caught dead without one that matches. She's been teaching for the last few years at Indiana [University]. She's definitely from the old school of what a prima donna should be.

When Warren Wilson and Shirley Verrett were at the New York airport — you know, Shirley Verrett is very chic ... looking like she just stepped out of *Ladies Home Journal*—[Verrett and Williams] greeted each other and Williams said, "Girl, you got to get yourself a fur coat!" And Warren screamed because Shirley was the epitome of chic. But that was the old way. "You a prima donna. You got to act like a prima donna. Get yourself a fur." Got real ethnic. "Honey, you got to get yourself a fur."

When I went to the University of Illinois she was already teaching over at Indiana. And after the second year I was [at the University of Illinois], the University of Indiana made some overtures and asked me would I come over and talk with them. They were interested in my joining the

Portrait of Portia White. Courtesy of the E. Azalia Hackley Collection, Detroit Public Library.

faculty, so on and so forth … And I went over and, of course, she and I got together and we were talking — she's very religious you know — and I said, "Well, have you decided? Are you going to be here for a while?" She said, "Well Warfield, I don't know." She said, "I'm praying on it. I'll have to let the Lord tell me what to do. I haven't made up my mind yet. He hasn't told me." So, I didn't think anymore of it. Later on I ran into John Motley. I said, "Oh, is Camilla going to stay at Indiana?" And he said, "Yeah." And then I told him this story. And I said, "Cause when I was there she wasn't sure whether the Lord wanted her to go back." He said, "Well, you know what happened don't you? They offered her five thousand dollars, she told the Lord to go to hell, and took the job." So she's been there ever since.

— *William Warfield, April 21, 1994*

On October 18, 1922, Camilla Ella Williams, the youngest of four children, was born to Fannie (Carey) Williams and Cornelius B. Williams in Danville, Virginia. Throughout her childhood she received extensive musical training at home, in church, and in school. So her decision to embark on a career in music after graduating from Langston High School was not much of a surprise.

In 1941 she graduated from Virginia State College and taught elementary school in her hometown of Danville. Her college choir asked her to join them for a concert in Philadelphia as soloist. She did so and subsequently returned to Philadelphia for further vocal study on a scholarship established for her by her college alumni group.

While in Philadelphia she studied languages at the University of Philadelphia in 1942, studied voice with Marion Szekely-Freschi, and was the recipient of the Marian Anderson Award in 1943 and 1944. To gain additional income she worked as an usher in a theater. After receiving the Philadelphia youth audition award she was soloist with the Philadelphia Symphony Orchestra on November 14, 1944. The following year Williams gave a concert, in December 1945, in Stanford, Connecticut. Metropolitan Opera soprano Geraldine Farrar was in the audience and encouraged Williams to pursue a career in opera. In 1946 she auditioned for the director of the New York City Center Opera Company, Laszlo Halasz. A contract with the company followed, and on May 15 she made her debut as Cio-Cio-San in Puccini's *Madame Butterfly*. Farrar proved to be an important influence on Williams, for the young singer wore Farrar's costume on the occasion of her opera debut. In addition, Farrar coached Williams on this and other roles which had been in her repertory in years past. Williams remained with the New York City Opera until 1954, singing many principle roles, such as Nedda in *I Pagliacci*, the title role in *Aida*, and Mimi in *La Bohème*.

She made her Town Hall debut on January 12, 1947, and made opera and concert appearances in the Caribbean Islands and Central America. In 1954 she went to Europe. She sang with the Sadler Wells Opera Company of England, appeared in Berlin, the Hague, and made her debut with the Vienna Volksoper. Williams was the first African American to appear with this company. Her numerous concert tours have taken her to North and South America, many Scandinavian countries, Germany, Austria, Italy, France, England, and Japan.

In the 1970s Williams returned to academia, teaching voice at Brooklyn and Bronx Colleges, and eventually at Queens College. In 1977 she joined the prestigious voice faculty of Indiana University's School of Music.

SOURCES

Turner, Patricia, *Afro-American Singers* (Minneapolis: Challenge Productions, 1977), 391–393.

Henry (Harry) Williams
(1850s–1930s or 1940s)

Henry (Harry) A. Williams, tenor, was born in Cleveland, Ohio, where he received his early musical training. Numbered among the local teachers with whom he worked was John Underner. He later went to Paris, France, in 1886 and studied with Delle Sedie and Sbriglia. A trip to London, England, followed, where he worked with the renowned Francesco Tosti, and Luigi Denza became his patron. For the majority of his time in London he lived in the home of Denza, becoming acquainted with many musicians of note. He eventually received a temporary appointment with the London Academy of Music as a voice teacher. Denza and Pollitzer were the directors of the Academy. For a brief moment Williams returned to Cleveland in 1888, giving recitals throughout the area. Upon his return to England he toured with the Frazier Quintet, a British concert company, in 1890. In 1903 or 1904 he returned to Cleveland again, this time making it his home, and organized his own voice studio. In 1903 Mrs. Harriet Gibbs Marshall established the Washington Conservatory of Music in Washington, D.C. Williams became the head of the voice department of that institution in 1912. While in Washington, D.C., he organized and directed the Washington Concert Orchestra, a choral society and symphony orchestra for the conservatory. Bernadine Smith was the concertmaster. At some point in the 1920s Williams became the director of music at Florida Normal School in St. Augustine. He finally settled in New York City in 1927; there he conducted another voice studio and gave concerts. The Harlem community, as "Dean of Afro-American voice teachers," gave a testimonial concert in his honor in June of 1938.

SOURCES

Cuney-Hare, Maud, *Negro Musicians and Their Music* (Washington, D.C.: Da Capo Press, 1936), 205.
Southern, Eileen, *Biographical Dictionary of Afro-American and African Musicians* (Westport, CT: Greenwood Press, 1982), 404–405.

Lawrence Winters
(1915–1965)

His real name was Lawrence Whisonant. He was one of the first blacks [consistently] in opera, and that was City Center Opera and he was at the Hamburg Opera. Now, when I got back [from the Army] in '46 and they [the producers] asked me to come down [to New York City] and audition for *Call Me Mister,* Lawrence was at my audition. He was doing the role on Broadway and they wanted his input ... So, I'm sitting in the back and I was totally green. He [Lawrence Winters] walked up and he said, "Don't you accept less than [such and such]." And that's what I did and they gave it to me. Now he didn't have to do that, you know. He didn't have to do that. And then we remained friends all through the years.

You know, one of his big roles was the king [Amonasro] in *Aida.* And do you know what his wife's name is? Aida! Her real name. He married a girl named Aida ... He eventually remained, most of the time, in Europe doing opera because, when he was doing his best operatic roles, the Met still wasn't open to blacks. Only in the middle fifties it started to open up and then it was mostly for women. Simon Estes [noted bass-baritone] said that if he'd been a woman, he would've been at the Met for a good four years before he [eventually] got there.

— *William Warfield, April 21, 1994*

Lawrence Winters (also known as Lawrence Whisonant) was born on November 12, 1915, in Kings Creek, South Carolina. His early musical education took place in the public schools of Washington, D.C., where Mary Europe encouraged the lad to study voice. He began his vocal studies in Salisbury, North Carolina, and eventually at historic Howard University in Washington, D.C. He studied with the noted African American baritone R. Todd Duncan at Howard and received his Bachelor of Music degree in 1941. Following his graduation he toured with the Eva Jessye Choir and made his New York operatic debut as Dessalkines in a concert production of *Ouanga,* an opera by the renowned African American composer Clarence Cameron White.

As a soldier during World War II Winters was director of music at Fort Huachuca, Arizona, in the Special Services Division. He also entertained. Lieutenant Winters began his postwar career as a nightclub singer and then in the Broadway musical *Call Me Mister* in 1946. He made 21 appearances in the West Indies during the summer of 1947, and made his Town Hall debut in New York in the fall of that year. Two Mexican tours followed. In 1948 he made his debut with the New York City Opera Company in Verdi's *Aida.* Winters played Amonasro. His repertoire at the New York City Opera included leading roles in *Carmen, The Love for Three Oranges, Troubled Island, Turandot, Rigoletto,* and *The Tales of Hoffmann.* Winters made his European operatic debut as Amonsaro at the Hamburg State Opera in Germany in 1952. He was principal baritone for the Hamburg Opera from 1961 to 1965. He toured Europe twice in such cities as Paris, Venice, Amsterdam, Zurich, Stockholm, and Berlin. He also toured

Portrait of Lawrence Winters. Courtesy of the E. Azalia Hackley Collection, Detroit Public Library.

South America, Central America, five of the United States, and Canada. He sang as guest at the San Francisco Opera and the Berlin City Opera.

Lawrence Winters was killed in an auto accident in Hamburg [?] on September 24, 1965.

SOURCES

"On the Front Cover," *Musical America*, April 15, 1952, 15.
Southern, Eileen, *Biographical Dictionary of Afro-American and African Musicians* (Westport, CT: Greenwood Press, 1982), 411.

Musical America, August 1950, 35

Telegraf (Berlin). The way Lawrence Winters filled Polyphem's aria from Handel's "Acis & Galtea" with dramatic expression cannot easily be equalled. Winters possessed a magnificent natural voice ...

Gazzetta del Popolo (Torino, Italy). Triumphal and well-earned success ... magnificent natural gifts; a voice like an organ, beautiful, vibrant and rich; uncommon technique.

Giornale di Brescia (Italy). The audience shouted its admiration for the Negro baritone ... it was a triumph ... perfect musicianship and style dominated and galvanized the program.

Ilta Sanomat (Helsinki). Lawrence Winters is a great artist; his expressive scope has no limits. The voice has a mellow, beautiful timbre. Vocal production is exemplary, without effort, and the breath technique is of a virtuoso.

Suomen Sosialidem Okraatti (Helsinki). Lawrence Winters has been compared with Paul Robeson and Marian Anderson, and truly, not without reason ... He owns a velvety vocal instrument, which he uses with supreme art.

Verdens Gang (Oslo, Norway). A splendid voice ... it rings with marvelous sonority ... tremendous success ... audience asked for encore after encore.

Aftenposten (Stockholm). Lawrence Winters' voice is as beautiful as one can ask for ... He masters it brilliantly. His vocal art bears the stamp of thoroughly musical culture.

Morgenbladet (Stockholm). His vocal interpretations are animated with such glow and joy that the listeners could not help being carried away ... His magnificent voice unfolded in full splendor — a heroic baritone with an imposing register and spellbinding quality. The treatment of the texts was masterly ...

Die Welt (Cologne). An exciting event ... An uncommonly rich vocal material is joined by perfect tonal culture and natural dignity of performance. Heart and intellect function in rare harmony.

Uusi Suomi (Helsinki). It is refreshing to listen to Lawrence Winter's natural voice production. One hardly notices breath-pauses, and the voice sounds natural in all degrees of volume. An artist of very great class.

Neue Zurcher Nachrichten (Zurich). The sonority, splendor and volume of this expansive, powerfully expressive voice can hardly be described with dry words. An unbroken, but restrained vigor and a vitality that carries away are evident.

Die Tat (Zurich). A voluminous voice, full of power and masculinity and of warmth that immediately speaks to the heart. With original musicality he sings Schubert, Wolf and Brahms in German, or Faure and Duparc in French, and subtly catches feeling and style of the songs.

Tages-Anzeiger (Zurich). To a German-speaking singer, who struggles with difficulties of declamation and other imperfections, one could not recommend a better model than this Negro baritone, who feels so much at home with Schubert, Brahms and Wolf as if he had never known another fatherland ... With amazing feeling for style, Lawrence Winters sang French songs (Faure and Duparc).

La Suisse (Geneva). The singer owns a voice which is full, supple, and of a perfect evenness in all registers. His articulation has a praiseworthy neatness. Aside from these advantages, Lawrence Winters possesses a wonderful sensitivity with which he interprets works of very diverse character.

Journal de Geneve (Geneva). One of the great singers of our time, most certainly not for a long time have we heard such a moving voice. A timbre of pure silk, sumptuous, deep, brilliant without hardness, as mellow in softness as rich in brightness, a tessitura of over two octaves ... an accomplished technique, an impeccably clear pronunciation in Italian as well as in German, French, or English. And he is an artist ...

Helsingin Sanomat (Helsinki). The singer has enormous vocal resources and excellent technique. His "forte" is extremely effective, his "pianissimo" insinuatingly beautiful.

Der Kurier (Berlin). It is hard to decide what filled Lawrence Winter's audience with more enthusiasm: the beauty of his sonorous voice, or his native power of expression. Whether he sings Handel arias or German and French songs, he always masters his extensive, fully flowing baritone.

"Winters Signed for *Lost in the Stars* Part," *New York Amsterdam News,* 1 March 1958, 12

Baritone Lawrence Winters will sing the leading role in "Lost in the Stars" which the New York City Opera will produce during its coming spring season of American opera.

Mr. Winters, who has just returned from Germany where he enjoyed a great personal success in opera, is foregoing a return engagement there this spring in order to do the role.

Jose Quintero who is presently directing Eugene O'Neill's "Long Day's Journey into Night," will direct the opera, which deals with race relations in South Africa.

"Winters Not Ambitious but Determined,"
New York Amsterdam News, 3 May 1958, 15

Lawrence Winters, the distinguished baritone who drew such warm praise for his acting and singing in the revival of "Lost in the Stars," would advise an aspiring artist to have determination but disclaim ambition.

"My ambition when I was studying at Howard University," admitted Winters, "was to sing at the Met. But then later I realized even if I did sing at the Met I would still be looking elsewhere and that would not be the end."

Although Mr. Winters had never been signed by the Metropolitan Opera C., he has sung from its stage. And his other lists of accomplishments are quite as imposing as some of the regular Met stars.

In Opera Companies. In addition to being a regular member of the New York City Opera Company since 1948, Mr. Winters is also a member of the Hamburg and Berlin, Germany Opera Companies and there's a good possibility he may sign with the San Francisco Opera Company this fall.

The present NYC Opera Company's production of "Lost in the Stars" was received so well that its engagement has been extended when the regular season ends from May 6–11.

It is a coincident that Mr. Winters is playing the part of the Rev. Stephen Kumalo, the part made famous in the Broadway production by his teacher at Howard University, Todd Duncan. Incidentally, he auditioned for the role in 1950 but was thought too young at the time.

Mr. Winters returns to Germany in June for some singing engagements and there's the possibility he may do "Showboat" or "Porgy and Bess" this summer.

As for the art of singing, Mr. Winters has some definite ideas.

"A singer," he says, "should always remain a student. Something can always be learned. The voice is nebulous. You can't put your finger on the trained mind."

"Caruso," he continues, "had to work every day. Flagstad says a singer is always a student as long as he keeps learning."

Mr. Winter does just that — keeps learning. He has come a long way since he left a little town in North Carolina called East Spencer and studied at Howard University in Washington, D.C.

But he continues to study. And to learn. And although he's not ambitious in the accepted sense of the word, he's determined.

Sidney Woodward
(1860–1924)

Sidney Woodward, tenor, was one of the most celebrated African American singers of his day. He was born on October 16, 1860, on a plantation, in Stockbridge, Georgia. He was orphaned at an early age and had great difficulty working his way through school. In 1889 a student of Frank E. Morge of Boston heard Woodward sing in Peoria, Illinois. With the assistance of the student, a Miss Clark, Woodward was able to receive formal vocal training from Morge in Boston. While in Boston he received his musical training from the New England Conservatory of Music where he studied with Edna Hall. In 1890 he sang professionally as a concert tenor, touring throughout the south. He used the funds accumulated from the tour to continue his vocal study. Lillian Nordica, a soprano with the Metropolitan Opera, heard Woodward about two years later and was instrumental in advancing his performing career. On February 15, 1894, he made his debut at Chickering Hall in Boston.

Philip Hale, writing of him in the *Boston Journal*, said, "He sings as a rule with ease, his tones are pure and well sustained, his attack is decisive, and he does not abuse the portamento; he knows the meaning of the word legato, he phrases intelligently, and holds himself in control, and his enunciation is admirable."

In 1893 Woodward also sang at the Chicago World's Fair on Colored American Day in August. In 1896, along with Inez Clough, Disseria Plato, J. Rosamond Johnson, and Belle Davis, he performed in John Isham's Oriental American Company. He was the principal singer in the part of the production called "Forty Minutes of Grand and Comic Opera." From the years c.1897 to 1900 Woodward studied in Germany and received a certificate from Dresden's Royal Conservatory. During this period he also performed in Russia, Belgium, Holland, Austria, Germany, Wales, Scotland, and Ireland. When he returned to the United States he set his sights on teaching. He taught at the Florida Baptist Academy in Jacksonville, Clark College in Atlanta, Georgia, and the Music Settlement School for Colored in New York City from 1916 to 1921. New York's leading African American musicians joined Woodward on December 19, 1921, at Carnegie Hall to celebrate his thirty-first anniversary as a concert artist. He died in New York on February 13, 1924.

Sources

Cuney-Hare, Maud, *Negro Musicians and Their Music* (Washington, D.C.: Da Capo Press, 1936), 231–232.

Southern, Eileen, *Biographical Dictionary of Afro-American and African Musicians* (Westport, CT: Greenwood Press, 1982), 413.

Discography

Key to symbols and abbreviations: *—Out of Print. #—Black Composer. ARG—American Record Guide. Col.—Columbia. DGG—Deutsche Grammophon Gesellschaft. E—Extended Play—45 RPM. Ed.—Edited, Edition. LP—Long-playing. MGM—Metro-Goldwyn-Mayer. No.—Number. ODY—Odyssey. Op.—Opus. RCA—Radio Corporation of America; RCA—Victor; RCA—Victrola. Rev.—Revised, Revision. RPM—Revolutions Per Minute. V-DISC—"...series of phonographic records produced during and after World War II by a small military group in New York ... were distributed to overseas military personnel ... 1943–49" (Sears).

Bledsoe, Jules

Bledsoe, *He Rose.* 75162 with orchestra. 78 RPM Issue: Royale 1701.
Bledsoe, *Does He Love You?* 75165 with orchestra. 78 RPM Issue: Royale 1702.
Burleigh, *Deep River.* 75166. 78 RPM Issue: Davis 8002B; Royale 1703.
White, *Wake Up Jacob.* 75167. 78 RPM Issue Royale 1701.
Robinson, *Water Boy.* F.3113 MXGB3664.
White, *There's a Man Goin' Roun' Askin' Names.* F3113 MXG3645.
Foster, *Massa's in de Cold, Cold Groun.* F3235. *Poor Old Joe. Swing Low, Sweet Chariot.* F3486. *Goin' to Shoul All Ober God's Heab'n.*
Bledsoe, *Does I Love You?* F.3852.

Brice, Carol

*Arlen, *Saratoga.* RCA LOC 1051, LSO 1051 [1959]. Role: Kakou.
Bach, *Sacred Arias.* Col. ML 4108 [1948].

173

Blitzstein, *Regina*. Col. 03L 260 [1959]. Col. 03S 202 [1959]. Role: Addie.
#Dett, *The Ordering of Moses*. Silver Crest TAL 42868 [197?].
*Falla, *El Amor Brujo*. Col. ML 2006 [1948].
*Franz, *Im Fruhling, Mutter, O Sing Mich Sur Rhue*. Col. ML 2108 [1952]. (A Carol Brice Recital) 10" 33-1/3 RPM.
Gershwin, *Porgy and Bess*. RCA ARL3-2109 [1977]. Role: Maria.
Mahler, *Lieder eines fahrenden Gesellen*. Col. ML 4108 [1948]. (Songs of a Wayfarer).
Richardson, *The Grass Harp*. Painted Smiles Records. PS 1354 [1971]. Role: Catherine.

Brown, Anne Wiggins

Gershwin, *Porgy and Bess*. Selections. DECCA DL 7006 10' 33-1/3 RPM [1950]. DECCA DL 8042 10' 33-1/3 RPM [1952]. DECCA DL 9024 [1955]. Reissued: MCA 2035 [197?] DL 79024. Role: Bess and Serena.
Gershwin, *Porgy and Bess*. Selections. Mark 56-667 [1974]. Role: Bess.
Burleigh, *His Word Is Love*. MX42050-1A. Emerson (Special Label) [1920].
Burleigh, *Go Down Moses*. No. 1. Broome Special Phonograph Record [1920].

Davis, Ellabelle

Opera, Leider. London LPS 181 [1950]. 10" 33-1/3 RPM.
Spirituals. London LPS 182 [1950]. 10" 33-1/3 RPM.

Duncan, R. Todd

Gershwin, *Porgy and Bess*. Selections. DECCA DL 7006 10" 33-1/3 [1950]. DECCA DL 8042 [1952]. DECCA DL 9024 [1955]. DL 79024e. Reissued: MCA 2035 [197?]. Role: Porgy and songs of Sporting Life and others.
Gershwin, *Porgy and Bess*. Selections. Mark 56-667 [1974]. Role: Porgy.
Weill, *Lost in the Stars*. DECCA DL 8028, DL 79120 [1950]. Role: Reverend Stephen Kumalo.
*Negro Spirituals: A Comprehensive Anthology, Allegro ALG-Elite 3022 [1951].
Spirituals. Royale 1810 [195?] 10" 33-1/3 RPM.

Hines, Altonell (Altonell Hines Matthews)

*Thompson, *Four Saints in Three Acts*. Abridged. RCA LCT 1139 [1954]. Reissued: RCA LM 2756 [1964]. Role: Commere.
Gershwin, *Porgy and Bess*. Col. 03L 162 [1951]. Reissued: Ody. 32-36-0018 [1968].

Excerpts: 10" 33–1/3 RPM Col. AL 31 [1953]. 12" 33–1/3 RPM Col. ML 47666 [1956]. 12" 33–1/3 RPM Col. CL 922 [1956]. Role: Jake.

Thompson, *Four Saints in Three Acts*. Abridged. LCT 1139 [1954]. Reissued: RCA LM 2756 [1964]. Role: St. Ignatius.

Holland, Charles

Williams/Henderson, *Harlem Madness*. 24699A Victor [1934]. MXBS81789–1–1. 78 RPM Issues: RCA Victor–RD7598 (Eng.) 130.429. 430.671; 730 (Fr.); LPM–10 121 (Ger.).

Johnson, *Honor! Honor!* 4556A.

Dawson, *Talk About a Child*. 4556B. *That Do Love Jesus*.

Blitzen, *The Airborne*. 11–9531 to 11–9537. MX11–9524 — MX119530. RCA Victor DM1117.

Thompson, *Four Saints in Three Acts*. 12–0456 to 12–0460. LP Issue: RCA LCT-1139 [1954]. RCA Victor LM2756 [1964]. MX12–0451 — MX12–0460. RCA Victor DM1244. *Argentine Folk Song Vidalita*, MXCO39905. 72812-D MM831. LP Issue: Columbia AAL22 [1949]. Columbia 1940s. *Go Down Moses*, 469-B / V-DISC 1944. *Walk in Jerusalem, Just Like John*. MXCP1327 249B. V-DISC 1944.

Matthews, Inez

*Beethoven, *Gellert-Leider*. Six Sacred Songs. Period SPL 717 [1955].

Gershwin, *Porgy and Bess*. Col. 03L 162 [1951]. Reissued: Ody. 32–360018 [1968]. Excerpts: 10" 22–1/3 RPM Col. AL 31 [1953]; 12" 33–1/3 RPM Col. ML 4766 [1954]; 12" 33–1/3 RPM Col. CL 922 [1956]. Role: Serena.

Gershwin, *Porgy and Bess*. Selections (Sound track). Col. OL 5410, OS 2016 [1959]. (Sang Serena, which was portrayed in the film by Ruth Attaway).

Schubert, Die Schone Mullerin. Op. 25 D. 795. Period SPL 713 [1955].

Schubert, *Schwanengesange*. Op. 89 D. 911. Period SPL 714 [1955].

Schubert, *Winterreise*. Op. 89 D. 911. Period SPL 714 and 1–7" [1955].

Thompson, *Four Saints in Three Acts*. Abridged. RCA LCT 1139 [1954]. RCA LM 2756 [1964]. Role: Saint Settlement.

Weill, *Lost in the Stars*. DECCA DL 8028m DL 79120 [1950]. Role: Irina.

Spirituals. Period SPL 580 [1953].

Maynor, Dorothy

*Duparc, *Phidyle and L'Invitation du Voyage*. Royale 49–1279 45 RPM [1950].

The Art of Dorothy Maynor. RCA LM 3086 [1969].

Spirituals and Sacred Songs. Camden 344 [1957].

Arias and Duets. RCA LCT 115 [1953]. *Critics' Choice*. RCA WCT 115 [1953].

Gershwin, *Porgy and Bess*. Selections (Soundtrack). Col. OL 5410, OS 2016 [1959]. (Sang Porgy, who was portrayed in the film by Sidney Poitier).

Classic Negro Spirituals. Washington 466 [1962].
Deep River and other Classical Negro Sprituals. Riverside RLP 12–812 [1959].
Verdi, Rigoletto. Selections: Metropolitan Opera Club Recording—M0214.

Mitchell, Abbie

Gershwin, *Porgy and Bess.* Selections. Mark 56 667 [1974]. Role: Clara.

Talbert, Florence Cole

Dell'Acqua, *Villanelle.* Broome Special Record [1919]. 9080B MX1410x. Black Swan
   Records [1923].
Delibes, *The Bell Song.* 7103A-B.
Arditi, *Il Bacio.* 7104A. (The Kiss).
Flotow, *The Last Rose of Summer.* 7104B 78 RPM. Paramount 12187B.
Del Riego, *Homing.* 12096A. Paramount [1924].
Eckert, *Swiss Echo Song.* 12096B. Paramount [1924].

Warfield, William

*Brahms, *Vier ernste Gesange.* Op. 121 (Four Serious Songs). Col. ML 4860 [1954].
*Copland, *Old American Songs.* Col. ML 2206 [1951].
Copland, *Old American Songs.* (Sets I and II). Col. ML 5897, MS 6497 [1963].
Gershwin, *Porgy and Bess.* Selections. RCA LM/LSC 2679 [1963]. Role: Porgy.
Handel, *The Messiah.* (Bernstein). Col. M2L 242 [1957]. Col. M2S 603 [1960].
Handel, *The Messiah.* Excerpts (Bernstein). *Christmas Music,* Col. ML 5300 [1958].
   Col. MS 6020 [1960]. *Easter Music,* Col. ML 5346 [1959]. Col. MS 6041 [1959].
Handel, *The Messiah.* (Ormandy). Col. M2L 263 [1959]. Col. M2S 607 [1959].
*Kern, *Showboat.* Selections. Col. OL 5820, OS 2220.
Kern, *Showboat.* Selections. RCA LCS/LOC 1126 [1966].
*Kern, *Showboat.* Selections. MGM-E 559 10" 33–1/3 RPM [1951]. MGM-K 45 RPM.
*Loewe, *Ballads.* Col. ML 4545 [1952].
*Mozart, *Requiem in D Minor.* K 626. Col. ML 4860 [1954].
*Schumann, *Liederkreis von Eichendorff.* Op. 39. Col. ML 5861, MS 6461 [1963].
Schumann, *Spanische Liebes-Lieder.* Op 138. Col. ML 5861, MS 6461 [1963].
Wiegl, K., *Songs.* Turnabout TV 34522 [197?].
Ancient Music of the Church. Col. ML 4545 [1952].
Deep River. Col. AAL 32 10" 33–1/3 RPM [1953].
God of Our Fathers. Capitol P 8578, SP 8578 [1962].
Sea Chanteys. Col. ML 2206 [1951].
Gershwin's Greatest Hits. RCA LSC 5501 [1971].
Spirituals, 200 Years of African American Spirituals. Pro-Arte Digital. CDD 3443
   [1993].

Williams, Camilla

Gershwin, *Porgy and Bess.* "Summertime." 46–0004B. RCA Victor Black Label
   [1940s].

O' What a Beautiful City, Red Seal. 10–1425A.
City Called Heaven. 10–1425B.
Mahler, *Symphony No. 8 in E Flat.* Off-the-Air Record Club. OTA 6. Penzance PR 19 [1973].
Verdi, *Aida.* Selections. MGM E 554 10" 33–1/3 RPM [1951]. Reissued: MGM E3023 [195?].
Songs. MGM E 140 10" 33–1/3 RPM [1952].
Spirituals. MGM E 156 10" 33–1/3 RPM [1952].
Opera's Greatest Hits. Col.
Gershwin. *Porgy and Bess,* Col. 03L 162 [1951]. Reissued: Ody. 32–36–0018 [1968]. Excerpts: Col. AL 31 10" 33–1/3 RPM [1953]. Col. ML 4766 12" 33–1/3 RPM [1954]. Col. CL 922 12" 33–1/3 RPM [1956]. Role: Bess.

Winters, Lawrence

Gershwin, *Porgy and Bess.* Col. 03L 162 [1951]. Reissued: Ody. 32–36–0018 [1968]. Excerpts: Col. AL 31 10" 33–1/3 RPM [1953]. Col. ML 4766 12" 33–1/3 RPM [1954]. Col. CL 922 12" 33–1/3 RPM [1956]. Role: Porgy.
Gershwin, *Porgy and Bess.* Selections. MGM 70095, S70095 [1959]. Reissued: Heliodor H/HS 25052 [1967]. Role: Porgy.
Leoncavallo, Pagliacci. Selections. DGG LPEM 19199.
Moore, *The Devil and Daniel Webster.* Westminster OPW 11032 [1958]. Reissued: Desto D 450, DST 6450 [1965]. Role: Daniel Webster.
*Rome, *Call Me Mister.* Decca DL 7005 [1950].
Tamkin, *The Dybbuk.* Phoenix IX [1974]. (Matrix No. S-1 LS 37, 47). E554 10" 33–1/3 RPM [1951].
*Verdi, *Aida.* Selections. MGM E3023 [195?].
*Verdi, *Nabucco.* Selections. Asco 106 [1961].
Verdi, *La Traviata.* Selections. DGG 136005. Reissued: Heliodor 2548–117.

Bibliography

Abdul, Raoul. *Blacks in Classical Music.* New York: Dodd, Mead, 1977.

Cuney-Hare, Maud. *Negro Musicians and Their Music.* 1921. Reprint, New York: Da Capo, 1974.

Daughtry, Willia Estelle. *Sissieretta Jones: A Study of the Negro's Contribution to 19th Century American Concert and Theatrical Life.* Ann Arbor, Michigan, 1968.

Dwight, John Sullivan. *Dwight's Journal of Music.* New York: Da Capo, 1974.

The Foundation for Research in the Afro-American Creative Arts, Inc. *The Black Perspective in Music.* Cambridge Heights, N.Y.: 1971.

Lovinggood, Penman. *Famous Modern Negro Musicians.* New York: Da Capo, 1978.

The New Grove Dictionary of American Music. New York: St. Martin's, 1986.

Simpson, Anne. *The Life and Music of Harry T. Burleigh.* Metuchen, N.J.: Scarecrow, 1990.

_____. *The Life and Music of R. Nathaniel Dett.* Metuchen, N.J.: Scarecrow, 1993.

Skrowronski, Jo Ann. *Black Music in America: A Bibliography.* Metuchen, N.J.: Scarecrow, 1981.

Southern, Eileen. *Biographical Dictionary of Afro-American and African Musicians.* Westport, Connecticut: Greenwood, 1982.

Trotter, James Monroe. *Music and Some Highly Musical People.* 1878. Reprint, New York: Johnson Reprint Corp., 1968.

Turner, Patricia. *Dictionary of Afro-American Performers, 78 RPM and Cylinder Recordings of Opera, Choral Music, and Songs, 1900–1949.* New York: Garland, 1990.

Warfield, William (with Alton Miller). *My Life and My Music.* Sagamore Publishing Company, 1991.

Index

Numbers in italics refer to pages with photographs